COMPANION HANDBOOK

FOR

LAW STUDENTS

What they don't teach you at Law Schools in India

NITIN POTDAR

INDIA · SINGAPORE · MALAYSIA

ISBN 979-8-89186-979-0

Contents

Justice R. Mahadevan
Judge

Supreme Court of India
New Delhi.

23rd August, 2024

FOREWORD

At the outset, I wish to congratulate the author, an established lawyer, to have taken up this project of helping young minds make crucial career decisions that will shape their own professional landscape as well as build the collective future of this country. The handbook has answers to virtually every question and apprehension that is likely to arise in the mind of an aspiring lawyer, including on whether at all he should choose law as a profession. This Handbook does this by allowing a potential lawyer to assess himself on his aptitude and appetite for the law, and his skills and strengths, both generally and professionally.

Being a lawyer for more than three decades, Mr. Potdar has been through the roller-coaster ride that this highly competitive profession offers. His own professional journey, stated with detailed anecdotes and experiences, are evidence to the zenith and nadir that the legal profession, that demands at its core, single-minded devotion, dedication, industry, and adherence to ethical principles, is all about. While everyone must walk their own path all by themselves, books like these are sure to illuminate the path of those who decide to start their journey on the same road. This work is a boon to all

Justice R. Mahadevan
Judge

Supreme Court of India
New Delhi.

those who would like to hear words of wisdom that can save many an aspirant from committing the oft-repeated mistakes made at the initial stage of the profession. The author has dedicated an entire chapter to 'Frequently Asked Questions', with as many as 100 questions in them. In fact, many students do not know whom to address these questions to and these can more appropriately be called– 'Frequently Pondered-upon Questions", to which this handbook offers a treasure-trove of answers. The book which holds a wealth of information, lucidly arranged, and capable of being processed easily, will be of priceless worth to students who seek career counselling, especially in the field of law.

Importantly, the book is a source of encouragement to many who struggle for recognition in their early days, inspite of their sharp acumen and industry. To all those, this book offers wise counsel and renewed motivation to discover that they are indeed- *"THREE FEET FROM GOLD".*

[R. Mahadevan]

Preface

As I begin to pen this preface in the aftermath of an unprecedented global crisis, my heart goes out to a generation of students whose academic and professional journeys were starkly altered by the COVID-19 pandemic. The year 2020, marked as the year of global lockdowns, brought the world to a standstill. A microscopic virus, the Coronavirus, didn't just freeze the bustling rhythm of our daily lives but also cast a long, uncertain shadow over the future of countless students across various fields, including law.

As the world slowed down during the lockdowns of 2020, I found myself on an unexpected journey of introspection, tracing the path from the days of my law education, internship for solicitors, and from an Associate in *Crawford Bayley & Co* (9 years) to becoming Partner of *Amarchand Mangaldas* (6 years) and finally joining as an Equity Partner in *J. Sagar & Associates* (19 years and counting) – three totally different law firms in terms of structure and working culture. This period of reflection was enriched by my engagement with Richard Bach's 'Jonathan Livingston Seagull.' This book, more than just a story, became a mirror reflecting my own life's journey. It reminded me of the importance of looking beyond the apparent limitations, a lesson I learned through my school days, my legal education, the highs, and lows of starting in law practice, and the invaluable experiences and mentorship that shaped my career as a corporate lawyer. This period of contemplation reinforced my resolve to share these insights and experiences with the future generation of lawyers through this book, aiming to guide and inspire them as they embark on their own professional journeys.

For over two years (2020-2022), the pandemic ravaged our normalcy, upending the educational systems and throwing the career prospects of many into disarray. I often find myself pondering over the plight of those IIIrd, IVth and V[th] year students who missed crucial opportunities for internships – those essential steppingstones in shaping a professional career. The recruitment processes across industries, including law, came to a near halt, leaving thousands of aspiring professionals in a limbo of uncertainty and anxiety.

As the world grappled with this new reality, the concept of 'online internships' emerged as a makeshift solution, a concept that many law firms continue to adopt. Yet, I cannot help but empathize with the mental trauma and hardships faced by law students during this period. The disruption they experienced is more than just a pause in their career trajectory; it's a challenge to their resilience and adaptability in unforeseen circumstances.

The backlog of opportunities is still massive, and the path to recovery seems long and arduous. Witnessing this, I felt a profound urge to extend a guiding hand through these challenging times. This book is my humble attempt to reach out to those law students embarking on their professional journeys, to the recent graduates who are about to begin their careers, and even to those who are striving to progress, aspiring to become partners in law firms or to rise as influential general and inhouse counsels. **Honestly, my inner wishful thinking is that this book also serves to empower and encourage young lawyers to commence their own journey, maybe in the form of a small boutique practice in any specific new domain and gradually grow into a full-fledged law firm of global size and significance.**

Being a corporate lawyer for more than two decades, I am extremely passionate about the idea of connecting India's thriving entrepreneurial landscape, including large and mid-sized companies, SMEs, MSMEs, and startups, with law schools. India's entrepreneurial talent is undeniable, driving our nation's growth and innovation, increasingly demanding good corporate advice on foundational agreements, structuring innovative business models, licensing technologies and brands, fund raising exercises and working out exit options. On the other hand, there's a passionate pool of law students eager to become corporate lawyers, but they often lack the necessary guidance and opportunities. It's time to bridge this gap, creating a symbiotic relationship. Imagine a network where businesses connect with law students, tapping into their legal expertise. This initiative would empower future lawyers with practical experience while providing invaluable legal support to businesses navigating complex regulations. It's a win-win, and I'm committed to making it a reality. In this book, I have outlined a detailed action-plan to connect law schools with industries via industry forums.

Throughout my career as a corporate lawyer, which began in a vastly different era, I have witnessed the transformative evolution of the legal landscape in India. In these pages, I have poured not just my knowledge and experiences but also my empathy and understanding of the unique challenges faced by today's law students and young professionals. **This book is a companion – a mentor in written form – aiming to bridge the gap between academic learning and the practical realities of the legal profession with a special focus on a career as a corporate lawyer.**

Furthermore, in these pages, I have taken the liberty to share in great detail my journey as a corporate lawyer, illuminating the intricate and often challenging pathways of this specific field. This narrative is interspersed with practical wisdom and experiences that I have accumulated over the years.

Additionally, recognizing the myriad challenges that law students and young professionals face, I have included a comprehensive section of almost 100 frequently asked questions. These FAQs address common concerns and dilemmas, offering guidance and clarity to those navigating through pivotal stages of their legal careers. Originating from my interactions with young, inquisitive minds, it is a dedication to the relentless quest for knowledge among law students, especially those from smaller towns and cities, who often commence their legal education without the guidance of a familial or social roadmap. **Additionally, I have identified certain actionable points that, if institutionalized by Law Schools and Law Firms, would certainly help young lawyers to progress in their careers.**

To the young minds reading this, remember that your journey in law is not confined to understanding statutes and case laws; it encompasses a broader vision of justice, ethics, and societal impact. It's about building a foundation that is as much about legal acumen as it is about character and perspective.

Welcome to a journey that transcends the traditional bounds of legal education. Welcome to a path that I hope will not only inform but also inspire you to carve your unique niche in the vast and dynamic world of law.

Yours Sincerely,
Nitin Potdar

Chapter 1

Brief History

1.1 Introduction

It is elementary to begin this handbook with a slice of history before we come to the moot point of the essence, credence, and challenges of Indian legal education and its pedagogy.

The inception of the Supreme Court at Fort William, Calcutta, in the year 1773 marked the birth of the legal profession in India. Needless to say, only English, Irish and Scottish barristers, advocates, and attorneys at law could appear and plead in court, and no Indian advocate was allowed in the court. In 1793, Lord Cornwallis authorized the *Sadr Diwani Adalat* to enrol pleaders in Bengal, Bihar, and Orissa. Subsequently, the Legal Practitioners Act of 1853 allowed barristers and attorneys to appear before any Company court and the Letters Patent of 1865 established the High Court in Calcutta with similar provisions being made for establishing the high courts in Bombay and Madras.

The dawn of 1879 saw the Legal Practitioners Act granting powers to the high courts to enrol lawyers for different courts and initiate disciplinary proceedings against them. Amendments to the Bombay and Madras high courts allowed law graduates to become advocates after passing the prescribed exam. It is pertinent to note that while an advocate could appear on the high courts' original and appellate side, the *vakil* could not do so until the Madras High Court removed this distinction in 1886. The demand for an all-India Bar saw the appointment of the Indian Bar Committee, following which the Indian Bar Councils Act, 1926, was enacted. This act established a Bar Council for each high court consisting of 15 members, including the advocate general as an ex officio member. In 1961, the Indian Advocates Act standardised the legal profession across India and set up duly elected bar councils at the state and central levels.

Late Professor N.R. Madhava Menon, a renowned and revered legal educator, has succinctly captured the historical landscape of Indian Legal Education in his seminal paper "The Transformation of Indian Legal Education", published by the Harvard Law School Program on the Legal profession. It will be pertinent to examine some of his incisive points on the history of reforms in the Indian legal education system.

The span from 1960 to 1980 saw many heartening developments: LL.B. was made a three-year post-graduate program, private sector law teaching institutions mushroomed in the country, a core curriculum of mandatory subjects was introduced in full-time and part-time law colleges, and a one-year post-LL.B. apprenticeship was made compulsory for practice. Much later, when the Bar Council of India strategized a model law school through a five-year integrated LL.B. curriculum, the outcome was the inception of the first National Law School at Bangalore in 1986, which paved the way for many National Law Universities in due course. On the face of it, this phase saw the participation of bar, bench, and academia in the management of legal education, as well as collaboration with foreign law schools.

The year 1991, the year of India's globalization proved a game changer for the Indian legal profession which led to increased demand for corporate and business lawyers amongst the Indian business community; also, due to foreign direct investment coming to India, Indian lawyers got the opportunity to learn international best practices whilst working closely with their international counterparts. Again, the span after 1991, although a turning point for the legal profession in terms of market opportunities, did little to enhance the quality of legal education in the country, particularly in the field of corporate laws. Although many of the above-mentioned developments were heartening, to date, there has been no significant initiative to improve the pedagogy of the profession which cannot be equated with a mere expansion of the curriculum. The partnership of bar, bench, and academic yet leaves a lot to be desired, and the influence of foreign law schools has not been reflected in the manner it should have, given the passage of time. The underlying idea behind the inception of national law schools was the creation and proliferation of competent lawyers to improve access to justice for the common man. This objective has not been met, given the undue corporatization of the legal profession in urban areas, leaving much to be desired about the delivery systems working at the grassroots and across governmental agencies. Equal justice is still a myth in a democratic country like India.

Legal pedagogy needs to incorporate the actionable insights of senior lawyers, judges, and in-house counsel but till today, there has been no proactive initiative from any institution to invite the experts to the classroom. Vacant teaching positions abound in law school after law school. In another depressing trend, the academically bright graduates do not opt for post-graduate studies and steer clear of teaching and research positions. Even the few who are inclined towards higher education choose to migrate to the West. Post-graduate legal education in India is yet deprived of the essential nutrients which does not augur well for the legal profession in India.

Some proactive law schools recruit teachers from abroad or get into credit transfer arrangements where students and teachers are exposed to different learning environments. But these are essentially 'band-aid' measures and can't condone the detrimental effects of mediocre faculty and ill-equipped pedagogy on the delicate fabric of the legal education system, as well as the legal profession.

In the sections that follow, the student of law will find a roadmap for making the most of his or her time in law school and beyond. Given the academia-industry gap that exists, it is imperative that the student makes a herculean effort to seek as much depth as possible at the right age and time and not leave it all for experiential learning at a later stage in life.

Until the late eighties, when the five-year law school programs were not a part of the Indian legal education system, mostly only lawyers' sons and daughters consciously took up law as their profession, taking over the mantle from the earlier generation. Thanks to the grooming they received at home, these heirs found it easier to navigate the twists and turns of their educational voyage and weigh the pros and cons of each decisive step en route to their career voyage in law. Most of the other students with post-graduate qualifications like M. Com, M.A. and even M.Sc., to some extent, were often clueless about their higher education prospects and many among them pursued law by default. Obviously, there were very few meritorious or genuinely interested students among the many who ended up pursuing law in this unthinking fashion. This influx of casual students was a serious problem facing the sphere of legal education.

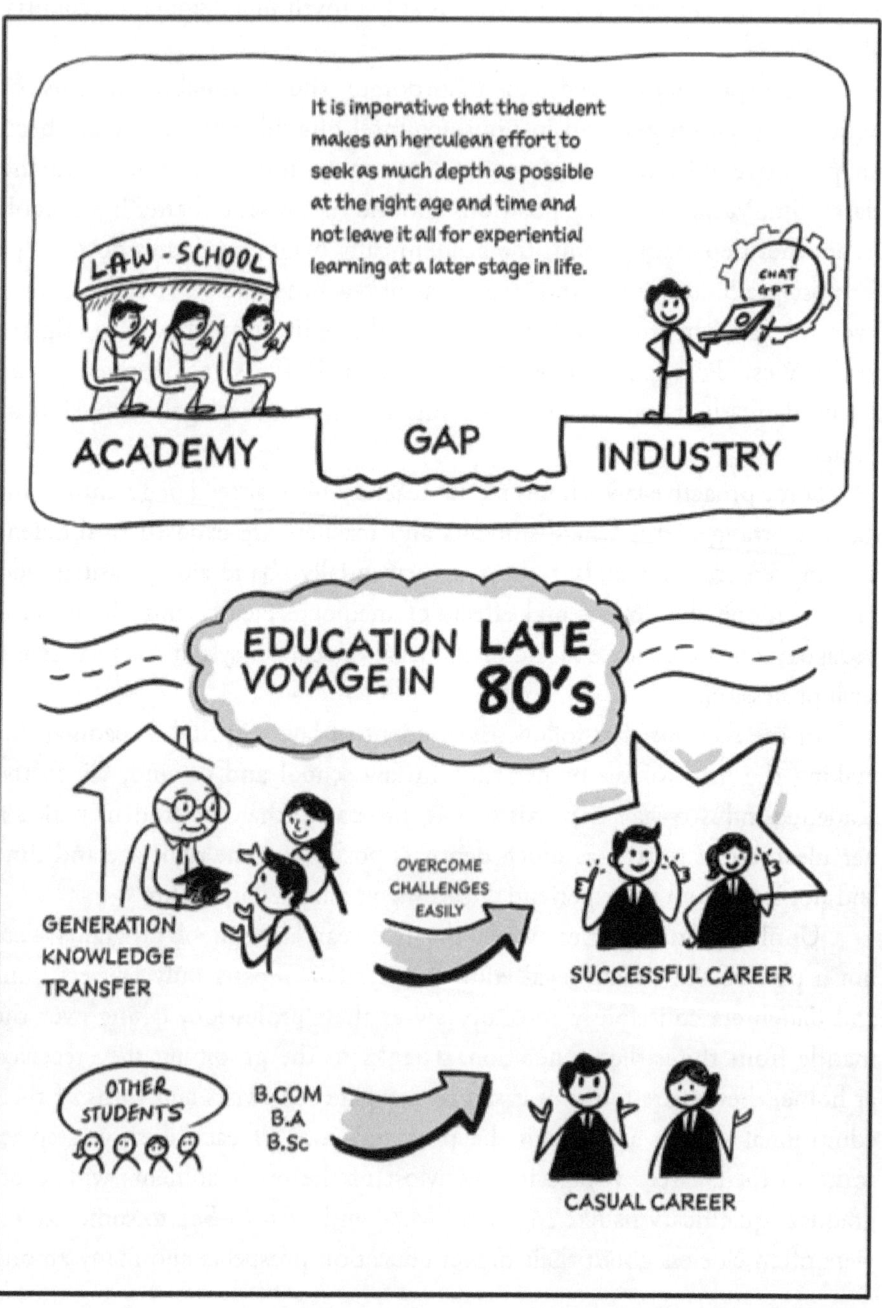

However, post-1988, more so after the 1991 wave of liberalization, things begin to change for the better. In 1989-90, the five-year law school program was introduced in India and coupled with the conducive environment of globalization, corporate law was adorned with a layer of glamour which vastly enhanced its market value. In the decade to follow, multiple law schools were incepted pan India and a common entrance exam was also formalized. There was a lot of buzz about foreign investment into the country which made corporate law a sought-after vocation along with finance.

1.2 Liberalisation of 1991

A flurry of legislative changes happened during this time starting with the NEP (New Industrial Policy 1991) introduced by the then Finance Minister Dr. Manmohan Singh. NEP brought sweeping changes in the form of (1) Industrial delicensing, (2) Deregulation of the industrial sector, (3) Public sector policy (de-reservation and reform of PSEs), (4) Abolition of MRTP Act, (5) Introduction of Foreign investment policy and foreign technology policy. The inception of SEBI in 1992 paved the way for a whole new career path in the form of Securities law. FERA (The Foreign Exchange Regulation Act, 1973) was replaced by FEMA (The Foreign Exchange Management Act, 1999), the Industries (Development & Regulation) Act 1951 was suitably modified, the MRTP (Monopolistic and Restrictive Trade Practices Act, 1969) was abolished and, in its place, a new Competition Act 2002 was brought into force. For the first time, people realised there is more to law than criminal law, property law and litigation matters. All of a sudden, corporate law seemed like a lucrative career choice, at par with medicine, engineering, or chartered accountancy. Consequently, even meritorious students scoring more than 90 per cent in their XIIth standard exams now turned to law, this time driven by a conscious choice.

Having said that, a fundamental flaw yet plagues the legal education system, which in my reckoning, has not been convincingly addressed. Every consultancy profession has its own demands which call for a specific mindset and temperament in addition to talent. I have my doubts as to whether a XIIth standard student does a thorough analysis of his or her capabilities in line with the demands of the chosen profession.

Let me elaborate on this point through an observation rooted in a comparative study of professions. It is very easy to enrol into a law course, compared to medicine or engineering, where the admission process is very stringent and calls for high stakes. However, it is extremely difficult to practice as a lawyer but comparatively easy to set up a medical or engineering practice. If you are an MBBS doctor with no experience, patients would still come to your door and pay you for the treatment received, simply by looking at your academic credentials on the name plate. In sharp contrast, you will still struggle to solicit business even if you are a gold medalist lawyer cand your nameplate proclaims so in bold letters. Even if prospective clients do land up at your door somehow, they won't consider your advice worth paying for if they come to know that you are a fresher with no experience whatsoever.

1.3 Practice of Law

Law practice in India refers to the profession of practising law. It primarily involves understanding facts and identifying issues, interpreting laws, advocating for clients, and applying legal principles to solve various issues. Lawyers in India may work in different areas such as criminal law, civil law, corporate law, property law and family law. They

represent clients in court, draft legal documents, and provide legal advice. Law practice in India is governed by the Bar Council of India, and lawyers must pass the All-India Bar Examination to practice. The profession also includes diverse roles like legal consultants, in-house counsel for corporations, judiciary, and roles in government services. Law practice in India is not just about court appearances; it also involves research, analysis, and continual learning to stay updated with legal developments.

Corporate Law: After 1991, corporate law practice involves guiding foreign companies on how to set up businesses in India be it a company, setting up partnerships/ LLPs or creating joint ventures/partnerships with Indian companies, and managing investments or technology agreements. Advising on business restructuring and obtaining court approvals for mergers, acquisitions, and demergers/spinoffs. It also includes helping Indian companies expand overseas. Lawyers in this field also assist Indian businesses of all sizes, including small and medium enterprises, startups, and LLPs. They help with creating commercial agreements or documents, getting funds from investors like private equity or venture capital, safeguarding intellectual property, and making sure companies follow all the rules.

The practice of law as aforesaid is a very intricate affair as every legal matter is different, and every case presents a specific problem. **The profession demands that you must be a solution-oriented person, open to fresh ideas and differing points of view, and above all, you must be a compulsive reader of the vast literature that abounds in the ocean of law.** There is no set process to follow, and you need to work around and innovate to the best of your ability and agility in conjuring a solution exactly in line with the facts of each case.

In medicine or engineering, solutions can often be found in textbooks, and it is largely a matter of diligent study and application of the amassed knowledge and experience to excel professionally.

PRACTICE of LAW
1 SOLUTION ORIENTED
2 COMPULSIVE READER
3 NO SET-PROCESS

Before taking up Law

My humble plea to all aspirants of law is to think deeply about what it takes to be a lawyer and introspect on whether they find themselves capable of delivering the goods in terms of the key characteristics. Each aspirant must ask himself or herself in the following order of priority:

- **Am I solution-oriented?** This is the first question one should ask before even thinking about studying law.

- Am I a good and careful listener?

- Do I relish considering a multitude of possibilities?

- Am I a good communicator?

- Am I willing to put in dedicated hours towards creating an objective and balanced solution?

- Am I a positive-minded person?

- Am I open to constructive feedback and diverse opinions?

- Am I okay with the fact that it may take many years to be successful as a lawyer?

I would urge every aspirant to deeply analyse his or her character, personality and bent of mind before taking the decisive plunge into the living waters of law. It is okay if your answers to some or all of the above questions are not affirmative, but it is important to acknowledge the need for adopting a positive frame of mind towards inculcating each of the above traits that are elementary for a career in law.

I would like to believe that Generation Z and Generation Alpha are much more tech-savvy. They do a detailed analysis of offbeat matters, like when they decide to spend 3 hours on a movie; they would first find out which Multiplex/Mall is showing the movie, and whether it is a 'cool' place in terms of food, shopping experience, and the ambience, so that they don't end up wasting their precious 3 to 4 hours of the given day. They spend phenomenal screen time on their cell phones to explore fashion trends, food joints, electronic gadgets, and exotic vacations. Strangely enough, the same lot of youngsters don't bother to do any research, let alone a detailed probe, before deciding to take the plunge into the living waters of a law school, or for that matter, to venture into any career stream. This idiosyncrasy is baffling, to say the least.

Legal education cannot thrive on a formulaic approach, nor is there a defined entry point to embark on a law career. It does not even presuppose a particular stream of secondary education, given that we have seen people from diverse educational backgrounds and career streams doing very well as legal professionals.

As regards the entry point, one can enrol for a law course following one's undergraduate studies without any work experience whatsoever. On the other hand, one can begin the tryst with the law at a much later stage as well, after having accumulated some industry experience across different spheres and walks of life. As the legal field thrives on a diversity of backgrounds, expertise, and even perspectives, classroom interactions actually become wholesome and outcome-oriented if students of different exposures form their core.

The legal profession may seem like a haven for easy-going professionals, but it is extremely difficult to survive and thrive in this highly competitive vocation. A gold medallist doctor can commence practice on day one as patients don't care about the doctor's experience, nor do they have any qualms about paying fees. In contrast, a gold medallist lawyer would not get even one brief to argue on his first day of practice, forget securing any fees.

1.4   Do an honest assessment of yourself.

Having said that, it is elementary to have a deep and abiding interest in law for any aspirant of this stream. A good starting point is an honest assessment of your areas of interest, core competence, and areas of improvement. Law demands the ability to analyse any given situation and find a practical and workable solution. And in doing so, you need to listen patiently to all concerned, understand the facts correctly, apply legal provisions, and articulate your thought process (verbal or written) with credible and compelling reasons in a simple and lucid language.

Don't go by your elders' perception which is often clouded by their vision, aspirations, and personal experiences. Do not fall victim to peer pressure or herd mentality either. Like how opting for a medical or engineering career because of what your parents want you to be is absurd, so is the case with taking up law because others you know have done so, or someone in your family has done so.

Parents (their ignorance and ego in particular) are often the biggest stumbling block in my opinion. I know of many parents plagued with preconceived notions about good careers who force-fit them to prescribe a stereotyped career path for their children. They want their kids to become 'graduates' at all costs, while the notions of an 'ideal' professional stream are already hardcoded in their minds. This is totally absurd. No wonder, hundreds and thousands of students switch to arts or music after passing medical or engineering.

Another hurdle in the way is the great Indian obsession with marks, grades, and family professions. Students' choice of career is yet largely dependent on the marks they obtain in Standard XII, as well as on the career choices of their parents or elder siblings or cousins. They feel it is easy to follow in someone's footsteps rather than find one's course in line with one's interests and competencies. **This is a monumental blunder in the context of a career** choice, especially in the context of the legal profession which is totally different from engineering or medicine, and I only hope that Generation Alpha would at least think seriously and find their own interests before they jump onto the bandwagon.

1.5   Appear for multiple aptitude tests

Ideally, students should appear for multiple aptitude tests and enrol for career guidance workshops right from VIIIth standard onwards. Things are improving on this front, albeit very slowly and only among affluent families. These days, online career counselling is gaining in popularity, but it is yet at a nascent stage. This may involve helping individuals identify their interests, values, strengths, and goals, and exploring different career options that align with these factors. In the Indian context, career counselling is particularly important due to the vast and diverse range of career options available to individuals across a wide range of sectors,

The idea, or the core purpose, of career counselling is to provide individuals with guidance and support in making informed decisions about their career paths.

including technology, healthcare, education, and manufacturing, among others. Indian students face a number of challenges when it comes to making career decisions, including a lack of awareness about different career options, limited access to career-related resources and guidance, and a shortage of skills and training opportunities in certain fields. Also, we need to address issues related to social and cultural expectations around career choices.

1.6 Career Counselling

Overall, the core purpose of career counselling is to empower students to take control of their careers and achieve their full potential at the workplace. The aim of these services is to help law students navigate the complex and competitive legal job market so that they can make an informed decision; and also, to assist them in developing the skills and experience needed to succeed in their chosen legal careers.

Career counselling services are provided by dedicated career services offices, which offer services such as resume and cover letter reviews, job search strategies, interview preparation, and networking opportunities. Some law schools may also offer mentoring programs, where students are paired with alumni or other legal professionals who can offer guidance and advice on career development.

In addition to these services, many law schools offer courses or workshops on career-related topics, such as legal ethics, professional responsibility, and career planning. These courses may be designed to help students develop the skills and knowledge they need to succeed in their chosen legal field. Overall, career counselling is an important component of legal education in both Europe and the US, that helps law students make

The biggest difference in Indian education vis-a-vis foreign education is that in the latter's case, students in Europe and US are compulsorily counselled before they pick their major subjects at the under-graduation level. Many law schools in Europe and the US offer career counselling services to their students.

informed decisions about their future careers and thereby, succeed in the legal profession.

It is, therefore, advisable to clear all misconceptions before one opts for a career in law. It is nowhere close to the glamorous world that films and TV serials portray on the big and small screens in the form of high-octane courtroom drama, plush offices, and lavish lifestyles.

Chapter 2

Roadmap To Enter the Legal Profession

As you stand at the threshold of the legal profession, remember that you're about to embark on a journey that is as noble as it is challenging. Law is not just a career; it's a calling to uphold justice, advocate for the voiceless, and be the change in a world that so often cries out for fairness and integrity. This path you're considering is not just about understanding statutes and precedents; it's about shaping the very fabric of society.

This book is your compass in this vast and often daunting legal landscape. It's designed to inspire, guide, and empower you as you navigate the complexities and triumphs of a legal career. From the fundamental principles of law to the unexplored niches of legal practice, we'll explore what it truly means to be a lawyer. You'll gain insights into not only surviving but also thriving in this field, turning challenges into stepping stones for success.

Let's embark on this inspiring journey together.

2.1 Research law schools

It is imperative to research various law schools to determine their culture and value proposition in line with your academic and future career needs. Nationally- or globally known law schools are best for students aspiring to work for large,

College Rankings: There's more to it than what meets the eye. Yes, college rankings do matter a lot, as a top-ranked college will provide you with a competitive edge in the job market. Having said that, you should not overlook critical factors like scope and relevance of college programs, bar passage rates, and quality of student bodies, which help in securing credible jobs.

international law firms, while smaller, state-based law schools are good choices for students hoping to make a career in that specific region. Do check out the prospects of getting into good law firms or with senior lawyers or even as a general counsel before firming up a law school. A good college will also have a dedicated placement cell to help you with internships. This is very critical if you have opted to become a good corporate, banking or securities lawyer or even disputes practice including arbitration or ADR.

2.2 Mentors and Eminent Lawyers: the key catalysts

Before embarking upon the journey of law school, one should ideally approach good lawyers, academicians, or mentors of the field to get actionable insights into legal education including its challenges, plus points, and certain harsh Indian realities. I may mention here that whilst in major cities like Mumbai, Delhi, and Bangalore the Corporate Law

Here, I would strongly recommend Law Schools/ Law Colleges organise free lectures of eminent lawyers/Judges/ partners from law firms for open public to create awareness about legal studies and publish this discourse on their YouTube Channels; or in collaboration with Junior Colleges or Schools Standard XII so that enough awareness is created about legal education and law practice.

Practice has gained prestige and is considered lucrative, in the two-tier cities law practice is mainly limited to lawyers going to courts for litigation for recovery of money or property disputes which is not what the next generation lawyers aspire for. It is, therefore, advisable to meet senior lawyers or to get a ringside view of the field. It is equally important to talk to law students about their experiences concerning the scope of the study, degree of stress and other hardships, etc. **In fact, not just law schools/law colleges, but even junior colleges should organize awareness campaigns during the course of XI and XII Std academic programs on different streams like Medicine, Engineering, Information Technology, MBA, Law, Accounting and other streams to help our young students make informed decisions.**

This inside information will help you decide whether you have the inclination and capacity to go through the grind. The rate of dropouts after two to three years is very common, and you should hence do your homework prior to enrolling for law rather than having second thoughts at a later stage. Make the most of networking websites/blogs and other forums which help you connect with law aspirants and professionals to seek personal guidance. This is important as medicine, engineering and a few other fields are well understood in India compared to the legal profession, which, for some reason, has remained an enigma to date.

2.3   Geography of practice: the epicentre of action

Some research on the key geographical regions of law practice can help you connect with the alumni networks and recruiting firms of those regions. The effort will give you a better idea of issues like average starting and median salaries, key industries, typical legal needs, major law firms, and professional organizations of the given area. This knowledge may help you secure a well-paying job with excellent prospects in a coveted geography. Venues like Mumbai, Delhi, and Bangalore have many good law firms, offices of MNCs and Indian corporate bigwigs, as also High Courts, institutions like SEBI, RBI, Stock Exchanges, Competition Commission, and TRAI which collectively offer a multitude of lucrative opportunities for law students for internships and placements.

2.4   Prepare for the CLAT and other Law Exams

As already discussed, securing admission to a recognised law school is the first and foremost step in your law career. Which law school you will join will be largely decided by your score in entrance exams and college GPA. There are various law entrance exams recognised and approved by Indian law schools. Hence, doing your homework is mandatory to get an idea of which law school you are aspiring for and which entrance exam you are required to take for that particular school.

These exams include CLAT (Common Law Admission Test, mainly for 5-year law courses), LSAT (Law School Admission Test, for both 5-year and 3-year law courses), University-based specific exams like SLAT (Symbiosis Law Admission Test) and AIAT (All India Admission Test) offered by institutes of Symbiosis International Deemed University, and state wise law entrance exams like Mah-CET (Maharashtra State Common Entrance Test), etc.

If your scores aren't anywhere close to where they should be, you can postpone the application process and first get the house in order by boosting your entrance exam score. Know which criteria are mainly judged in an exam. E.g., The Common Law Admissions Test, or CLAT, is a standardized test mandated by most law schools. The CLAT tests your logic, reasoning, analysis, reading, comprehension, and writing abilities. Since CLAT prep courses and materials are widely available, make the most of them and improve your chances of a higher CLAT score.

2.5   Cost/benefit analysis and job market realities

The per year average tuition fees of the top 10 national law universities is INR 2,60,000 per year (NLU Bangalore INR 2,88,855, NLU Delhi INR 1,86,000, NLU Hyderabad INR 2,52,000, NLU Kolkata INR 1,96,000, NLU Gandhinagar INR 2,69,000) Among private schools, the average fee is INR 3,50,000 (Symbiosis Law School INR 3,80,000, Jindal Global Law School INR 6,00,000, Amity Law School charges INR 3,00,000, etc). Please do check the current numbers from their respective websites.

Add to that accommodation and mobility expenses to pursue campus education. Bear in mind that you will not earn a steady salary for five long years in case you opt for practising in two-tier or three-tier cities and that too in litigation practice. Students' life in Mumbai could be slightly costly compared to other Metro cities.

Now, have a look at the average corporate lawyer's remuneration: This is the most uncertain area and may continue to differ from place to place. They come to INR 5 to 6 lakh per annum (2023-2024) depending upon the city you wish to practice. Freshers in some big corporate law firms in Mumbai, Delhi and Bangalore earn around INR 8 to 12 lakhs per annum on average (2023-2024). The exact figure depends on the base salary, shared profit, and incentive bonus. To cite a case in point, the Madras High Court average salary for a professional working under a senior is INR 7,000 -14,000 per month. In the Delhi High Court, it is INR 13,000 – 26,000 per month. Unfortunately, there is no standard remuneration package or minimum amount that one could expect as a fresh lawyer. And I don't see this situation improving in the near future. One should bear in mind that the legal profession is purely an experience-based profession. The more experience one gains, the more the remuneration and market value of your expertise. Senior advocates charge a minimum of INR 5 to 8 Lakh per appearance, and the maximum charge can touch the magic figure of INR 1 crore per appearance. So, the range of earnings is huge and at many times, misguiding.

Given this backdrop, you should be absolutely sure of your decision to opt for law and pave your path as realistically as possible. Look for law schools which publish statistics or share information about the jobs their graduates find after graduation. It is advisable to scout for schools where most graduates are likely to fetch full-time, long-term legal jobs in good time after graduation. If you find many part-timers or short-term job takers among pass-outs of a law school, it may not be the best place to build your foundation of legal education, especially if you have the burden of education loans and family responsibilities on your shoulders.

Chapter 3

Life in Law School

Student life is the soul of the learning endeavour and the effort one puts in at this formative stage in life reaps rich dividends later in life. Among other things, the student must bear in mind the following cardinal rules:

3.1 Classroom Attendance & Study Circles

Classroom attendance is a must to capture the insights a teacher is likely to share only while 'in the flow'. Attendance should not become a mere formality but a conscious endeavour to participate in the learning process by asking questions, listening to different viewpoints, and reviewing class notes. It is a good idea to gauge the teaching style of each professor and accordingly decide the extent of note-making. Some professors are in the habit of dictating notes, while others believe in freewheeling discussions. Some believe in reviewing lessons, others do not. Either way, your focus should be on capturing the key points of the subject and proactively asking questions to clear doubts and misconceptions. I must mention here that it is possible that on a given topic, the concerned faculty may not be fully prepared or well-read or the majority of your colleagues may not be aware of that topic, and you somehow have got the latest insights on that topic. It does not mean that you should unnecessarily try to show your superiority. **Be humble and polite in sharing your knowledge.**

Don't make it an ugly display of arrogance! Any discussion in the classroom is not a competition to be won!

Remember, the support of your Law school faculties and friends is extremely important in your journey as a lawyer and you don't want to make enemies right from the beginning of your career.

3.2 Institutionalise Study Circle of like-minded students

In the dynamic world of legal education, the concept of informal study circles could emerge as a powerful tool for enriching learning experiences. Why should law students engage in these circles? The answer lies in the multifaceted benefits they offer. Study circles encourage extensive reading and research, fostering a deeper understanding of legal principles and their practical applications. They become a platform for vibrant discussions, where students not only articulate their thoughts but also develop active listening skills, a crucial aspect for any budding lawyer.

But what exactly are these study circles? They are small, self-organized groups of students, ideally 5 to 6 in number, who could meet regularly to discuss various legal topics and case studies. This format ensures a personalized and engaging learning environment, where ideas can be exchanged freely, and diverse perspectives can be appreciated.

How can these circles be implemented effectively? The way forward involves institutional support from law schools to facilitate these groups, providing resources and guidance while allowing students the autonomy to explore topics of their interest. By institutionalizing study circles, law schools can significantly enhance the learning journey, making students not just better lawyers but also well-rounded individuals with a strong professional network and collaborative skills. The study circle, thus, becomes a crucible for nurturing future legal professionals.

Law Schools should encourage formation of such informal study circles on various topics and in fact institutionalize the process to incept a culture of open discussions, sharing insights and robust teamwork. And who knows, perhaps one day, this study circle might evolve into a small boutique law firm – what a fantastic way to kickstart a career after law school!

3.3   Internships: Real-Life Experience and Career Exploration

For law students, an internship is not just a phase; it's a deep transformative journey. It's where textbooks meet reality, where theories are tested, and where the seeds of a legal career are sown. Embrace each internship as an opportunity to learn, grow, and step closer to the lawyer you aspire to be. In these experiences, you'll find not only knowledge and skills but also your unique path in the vast world of law. Let each internship inspire you, challenge you, and guide you towards your future in law. Don't close your minds to civil or criminal practice as the final career path. Be open to understanding, exploring, and experimenting and then, choosing whatever you think is appropriate for you.

During your first- and second-year law school try to get internships and research work under individual senior lawyers, judges, or academicians, and from the third year onwards, one can explore internships with law firms. If for some reason you are unable to

During the first two years at law school, focus on getting really good at reading and understanding law. It's like learning the rules of a game – the better you know them, the better you can play! Get into the details, see how laws apply in real life, and train your brain to think like a lawyer.

get such internships, don't worry. This isn't just about memorizing stuff; it's about becoming sharp, smart, and ready to tackle any legal puzzle. Trust me, these skills are your secret superpowers in the law world. So, dive in, enjoy the learning, and build a rock-solid foundation for all the exciting challenges ahead.

I am aware that getting internships in big law firms is becoming increasingly difficult due to the large number of students applying for the available seats. Also, getting an internship in a particular practice area is also a challenge as many law firms don't offer practice-wise internships, for example corporate, banking, or disputes practices.

Remember, every internship is a golden opportunity. So, treat it with the seriousness it deserves. Always be proactive, polite and ready to learn. Dress like you're already an associate – professional and sharp. Being punctual and disciplined goes a long way to making a good impression. And guess what? If you look at the part, you might even get to tag along to professional meetings. That's a chance to see law in action and learn from the best. So, embrace every moment of your internship, and show them the star lawyer you're on your way to becoming. I am sure you will have scores of questions about internships. Let me preempt them and try to answer them one by one in the coming chapters. I may only repeat that an internship is a crucial stage in building your career in law. So, take it as seriously as you can.

Before you even step into the law firm for any internship, do your homework. Find out what they specialize in, their work culture, and their expectations, if any. Many law firms have detailed instructions for internship given on their website; read them carefully so you don't make any mistake. Internships often last just 4 to 6 weeks, which isn't a lot of time, so you need to hit the ground running. From day one, be eager to take on any task, no matter how big or small, and don't shy away from putting in those extra hours. Take notes whilst the seniors are instructing on the work including timelines for delivery so that you don't miss it. You never know which assignment might be the one that shapes your career. Make sure you seek some time with the senior partners to talk to them for some insights. Don't forget that everyone of us have undergone the same grind!

3.4 Law School Internship Cell:

The Internship Cell in law schools is not just a functional unit; it's a crucial bridge to the professional world. It's imperative that law schools take setting up their Internship Cells seriously, as they play a pivotal role in shaping the practical skills and career trajectories of aspiring lawyers. These cells are the gateways through which students step into the real-world legal landscape, gaining invaluable hands-on experience and professional insights. By fostering strong industry connections and providing diverse internship opportunities, these cells can significantly enhance the employability and readiness of law students for the challenges of the legal field.

Ideally, every law school should have a robust internship cell which should be supervised by any faculty member and a team of enthusiastic students. The internship cell should:

- Keep a comprehensive database of students with the facility to update their CVs on a regular basis,

- Have information about law firms (various practices), individual partners (their specializations), institutions like (SEBI, RBI), senior lawyers, judges, tribunals and their contact details.

- Have information about Industry Chambers/forums to establish connections with Large and Midsized business houses/MNCs/Startups.

- Have information about International law firms/Global Institutions that could offer internships.

This Internship Cell should act as the connector between students and the law firms/lawyers to help applicants secure good internship experience. Ideally, the Internship Cell should have strong leadership and administrative support who could constantly be in touch with the outside world and create opportunities for internships for their students.

There are ready software programs/web applications that would help set up an automated platform easily and cost-effectively.

3.5 Structured Internship programs by Law Firms

Internships are a vital aspect of a law student's journey, offering a glimpse into the dynamic world of legal practice. Law firms, recognizing this, can greatly contribute to shaping the future of the legal profession by offering a variety of internship options. These could include:

(a) Traditional summer internships, where students immerse themselves in the day-to-day workings of a law firm

(b) Project-based internships, focusing on specific cases or research areas

(c) Structured internships or select students from law schools

(d) Virtual internships, catering to the digital age and flexibility, and

(e) Pro-bono internships, where students contribute to community service and gain experience in public interest law

A well-structured internship program is a win-win for law firms. By investing in such programs, firms not only cultivate a pool of potential future lawyers who are already familiar with their work culture and methodologies but also enhance their own reputation in the legal community. Interns bring fresh perspectives and new ideas, fostering innovation and staying abreast of the latest legal trends. Furthermore, interns can assist with research and administrative tasks, increasing the firm's productivity. Most importantly, by mentoring young aspiring lawyers, the firm contributes to the development of the legal profession, creating a legacy of expertise and ethical practice. These interns are excellent brand ambassadors of the law firms and could certainly be the best tool for future business development.

Here are a few suggested internship programs that law firms could commence depending on their internal thought process:

- **GAIN** (Guided Apprenticeship in Law): A program focused on providing structured and guided legal experiences to law students.

- **RISE** (Research and Internship Skills Experience): Emphasizing both legal research and practical skills development through internships.

- **PACE** (Professional Apprenticeship and Career Experience): A program designed to set the right pace for a student's legal career through practical apprenticeships.

- **STEP** (Skills Training and Experience Program): Offering students the opportunity to step into the legal world and gain practical skills and experience.

- **PATH** (Professional Advancement and Training in Law): Aimed at guiding law students on the path to professional growth and success in the legal field.

- **LEAD** (Legal Education and Apprenticeship Development): Aimed at developing future leaders in law through education and apprenticeships.

- **FOCUS** (Fellowship and Opportunities in Court and Legal Understanding Systems): Concentrating on providing opportunities and fellowships in various legal systems and court procedures.

- **ACT** (Apprenticeship and Career Training): A straightforward program for apprenticeship and training to act effectively in legal careers.

Each type of internship serves as a unique learning platform, helping students hone their skills, understand different facets of legal work, and ultimately, decide their career paths in the diverse world of law.

Interestingly, Global law firms have set a high standard in this regard, offering a range of internships that not only benefit the students but also the firms themselves. Students gain practical experience, exposure to international legal practices, and networking opportunities, which are instrumental in their professional development. For law firms, these internships are opportunities to scout for talent, bring in fresh perspectives, and foster a connection with the next generation of lawyers. They also benefit from the innovative ideas and contemporary knowledge that students bring, often leading to improved legal strategies and solutions. This symbiotic relationship between students and firms significantly contributes to the ongoing evolution and success of the global legal industry.

3.6 Industry/Business Connect

Connecting India's thriving entrepreneurial landscape, including large and mid-sized companies, SMEs, MSMEs, and startups, with law schools is crucial. India's entrepreneurial talent is undeniable, driving our nation's growth and innovation. On the other hand, there's a passionate pool of law students eager to become corporate lawyers, but they often lack the necessary guidance and opportunities. It's time to bridge this gap, creating a symbiotic relationship. Imagine a network where businesses connect with law students, tapping into their legal expertise. This initiative empowers future lawyers with practical experience while providing invaluable legal support to businesses navigating complex regulations. It's a win-win, and I'm more than willing to assist law schools in making it a reality.

In Western countries, law schools place a strong emphasis on fostering connections between the legal industry and academic institutions. This mutually beneficial relationship is nurtured through various initiatives. Law schools often invite general counsel and industry experts to deliver guest lectures, participate in panel discussions, and mentor students.

Internship programs are designed to provide hands-on industry experience, allowing students to apply their classroom knowledge in real-world settings. These connections not only keep the curriculum updated with the latest industry trends but also offer students valuable networking opportunities and insight into practical legal work. For the industry, this collaboration is a chance to shape future lawyers and identify potential talent early on. Easy steps to facilitate this include, establishing formal internship programs, hosting regular industry-academic events, and creating mentorship schemes where professionals guide students in their career paths. The key advantages are a more industry-relevant education for students, better employment prospects upon graduation, and a continuous flow of fresh perspectives and innovative ideas for the legal industry.

I strongly recommend that law schools take the initiative to establish partnerships between academia and industry via various industrial forums and associations to create meaningful internship opportunities, workshops, and mentoring programs. This synergy fosters a win-win scenario, empowering the next generation of lawyers and providing invaluable support to businesses navigating complex legal terrain. Let's bridge this gap and witness the mutual growth and learning that follows.

3.7   Preparing a CV for an internship

Preparing a proper CV is the first step towards getting a good internship: (precise and powerful) and updating the same from time to time is extremely important for the purpose of securing an internship or later placement in any law firm, Company, or Institution. You need to spend good quality time learning how to prepare a smart CV. Maybe, you need to prepare two versions of your CV (one long form and another short one) and keep updating it for future use.

Look and feel of your CV

Your CV should be a Microsoft Word document, and you need to maintain **font uniformity** for all words. Don't keep the fonts too large, always keep them around 11. It is extremely important to have an accommodating **layout** where you can put up all your key information. My suggestion on the choice of fonts or layout may sound trivial  but trust me, a majority of CVs that I see suffer from extremely poor layouts. Nowadays on the internet, there is a plethora of ready-to-use CV templates. You just need to fill up the information using the template of your choice. However, do take care that the **basic design** is not too inventive as it might look unprofessional. It should look decent and proficient so that it will be easier for the person who is planning to hire you to form the best opinion about You. Use precise tabular formats to put all educational details from School to Masters in the middle page to highlight the content effectively. Convey content through bullet points instead of long paragraphs to enhance readability.

Make sure you have mentioned all **personal data** such as full name, date of birth, email address, the location of current residence, experiences, education details, achievements, hobbies and the like. Nowadays, employers also ask for a passport-size photograph.

Add a Statement of Purpose (SOP) wherein you write to explain why you want to do a law internship and why you are a good fit for the position. It could be in the form of a cover letter, or even one para in the main CV, but it focuses on your motivation, qualifications, and relevant experiences.

An SOP is important because it gives you an opportunity to showcase your interest in the legal profession and explain how an internship fits into your career plans. It allows you to tell the employer why you are excited about the opportunity, and what you hope to gain from it. If you cannot make up your mind on SOP, just leave it. Don't write for the sake of writing it.

In addition to explaining your motivation, an SOP allows you to highlight your qualifications. You can talk about your academic achievements, extracurricular activities, and any prior experience you have in the legal field. This information can help you stand out among other applicants and convince the employer that you have the skills and experience they are looking for.

Overall, an SOP is an essential tool for law internship applications because it allows you to present a clear and compelling case of why you are the best candidate for the position. A well-written and persuasive SOP can increase your chances of being selected for an interview and ultimately, securing the internship. But remember to be simple, precise, and honest.

How long should the CV be?

There is no absolute rule for the length of the CV as it depends on the data. It can be a one-page or two-page CV as per your data. Most people prefer a maximum two-page CV. It would be good if the CV is on an A4 size page with both-sided content. If the CV is too long, the recruiter may lose interest midway which can prove fatal. Making it precise can be an advantage as the organization can easily cull out the necessary information. Make sure all key matters are mentioned first.

To whom should one make an application for an internship?

I really get surprised when I see students sending CVs to all the Partners of any firm (and all are copied), or to Managing Partners of multiple law firms (again all are copied) without the slightest application of mind. This is completely suicidal! **Please do a little research on the law firm before you even think of making an application for an internship. This would give you a good idea of how to apply but the majority of applicants fail to do any homework and they keep sulking and finding faults with the law firms.**

Many Law firms today offer online application facilities for internships, which work well. It is just that the law firms get literally inundated with applications, and hence, your turn may not come easily, and you may feel frustrated. **Also, the majority of law firms have an HR Department wherein if you call up, they will explain the process and may guide you on the possibility of getting an internship.** Or you may just want to drop an email to the concerned partner from the relevant practice and seek his/her guidance. I also get surprised when law students apply for internships for intellectual property, tax or labour practice or any such practice despite knowing that the law firm does not have that practice at all.

As a Law student, what should be your email id?

I am sorry to take this up, but I find weird email IDs of students applying for internships or for job placement. In today's digital age, your email ID is often your first impression in professional circles. It's surprising how frequently this detail is overlooked. An email address that sounds casual or whimsical might be fine for personal use, but in the professional realm, it speaks volumes about your seriousness and professionalism. A simple, straightforward email ID, ideally a combination of your name or initials, conveys a sense of professionalism and reliability. It's a small but significant step in establishing your personal brand and credibility, especially in fields like law, where professionalism is paramount. **Remember, your email ID is not just a way to communicate; it's a reflection of your professional identity.**

Day one of an internship at a law firm:

Day one of any internship is a blend of excitement and nerves, a pivotal moment marking the beginning of a practical journey in the legal world. As you step through the firm's doors, there's an air of anticipation, mixed with the responsibility of making a great first impression. The day typically starts with introductions to the team, a tour of the office, and an overview of the firm's culture and practices. It's a day of absorbing new information, from understanding the firm's areas of specialization to learning about ongoing cases or projects. You'll likely be assigned a mentor or supervisor, who will guide you through the initial stages of your internship. There's an eagerness to demonstrate your eagerness to learn and contribute, coupled with the realization that this experience is a significant step in shaping your future legal career. The day often ends with reflections on the learnings of the day and anticipation of the journey ahead.

3.8   Alumni Association of Law School

The significance of a robust alumni association for a law firm cannot be overstated. Such an association serves as a vital link between the firm's illustrious past and its dynamic present, fostering a sense of continuity and community. Alumni, with their diverse experiences and accomplishments, form an invaluable network that not only enhances the reputation of the law school but also acts as a reservoir of mentorship and opportunities for current students. This network becomes a source of shared knowledge, experiences, and even potential engagement, strengthening the law firm's market position. Moreover, an active alumni association contributes to a culture of loyalty and pride, creating ambassadors for your law schools. Through events, newsletters, and mentorship programs, these associations keep former colleagues connected, not just with each other, but with the law school's evolving narrative, ensuring a lasting and mutually beneficial relationship.

Find out if your law school has an active alumni association where you are currently studying. If not, I would strongly recommend you consider establishing an alumni association for your institution. These are opportunities to showcase your leadership and teamwork at an early age.

Since I know law schools in India have not done much proactively to bring their alumni back to law schools, I believe it's crucial that current law students take this initiative seriously.

It's needless to mention that alumni associations serve as treasure troves of opportunities. By setting one up, you open doors to internships, job placements, and invaluable career guidance from those who've walked the same path.

It would help you to connect with former students who are now seasoned professionals in the legal field. Their experiences and insights can be priceless for your journey.

Here is a Stepwise Action Plan:

- **Step 1: Identify Enthusiastic Peers:** Rally like-minded students who share your vision. And you don't need more than three or four to begin with.

- **Step 2: Engage Faculty Support:** Seek guidance and support from your professors. Again, you just need one or two faculty members or talk to the principal.

- **Step 3: Create an Alumni Database:** Start compiling contact information of alumni from the college records.

- **Step 4: Plan Inaugural Activities:** Host alumni gatherings, workshops, or webinars.

- **Step 5: Digital Presence:** Set up a dedicated alumni website or social media group. Or simply create a WhatsApp group to begin with.

- **Step 6: Regular Updates:** Keep alumni informed about events and opportunities.

- **Step 7: Seek Alumni Feedback:** Continuously improve to meet their needs.

Alumni associations: Bridging the past, empowering the future!

3.9   Legal Lens on Social Media

In an era where digital footprints are scrutinized, it's crucial for law students to be acutely aware of their social media presence. The content you post, share, or even interact with can reflect your judgment, values, and professionalism. Therefore, it's not just advisable but imperative to maintain a dignified and responsible social media persona. Thoughtless, impulsive, or inappropriate posts can raise serious questions about your discretion and suitability for a career in law. Remember, in the legal field, reputation and integrity are everything. Your social media profiles shouldn't undermine these critical professional assets.

Recruiters and law firms invariably review social media profiles as part of their background checks, seeking insights into a candidate's character and suitability for the legal profession. In fact, I know law firms and many large companies hire professional firms to get a complete social media assessment on the candidates before recruitment is done.

In addition to the content of your social media posts, the images you choose to share, especially your display picture (DP), speak volumes about

your personal brand and professional image. As a law student or an aspiring legal professional, it's vital to recognize that these images contribute to how you are perceived by potential employers, colleagues, and clients. Your DP and other shared pictures should reflect a sense of professionalism and maturity. Avoid using casual or inappropriate images that could be misconstrued or send the wrong message about your seriousness towards a legal career. **Remember, in a field where perception often equals reality, ensuring your social media imagery aligns with the professional image you wish to project is not just important—it's essential.**

In today's era of unrestricted expression, my advice on being judicious with social media images and posts might not sit comfortably with everyone, especially students accustomed to a freer environment. However, I cannot stress enough the importance of this guidance in my book. It's essential to consider how your online persona might be perceived by those in the legal profession. I often encourage students to put themselves in the shoes of seasoned lawyers, recruiters, or senior partners. Imagine how they might view your social media presence. Would they see a promising, professional future lawyer, or someone who may not take their career seriously? This perspective shift is crucial in understanding the long-term impact of your digital footprint on your career prospects.

3.10 Writing Research Papers

Embarking on the journey of writing research papers as a law student is more than an academic exercise; it's an adventure in intellectual growth and skilful expression. Initially, start writing small pieces summarizing good Supreme Court or High Court decisions, and analysis of any newly introduced law, regulation or any amendment. This endeavour is not just about fulfilling course requirements; it's about diving deep into the ocean of legal knowledge, exploring diverse perspectives, and surfacing with valuable insights.

The process of writing research papers is a cornerstone of your legal education. It compels you to engage rigorously with complex material, sharpens your analytical skills, and polishes your ability to

Ideally, law students should form small peer groups to discuss topics and issues regularly. These discussion groups are like assembling a think tank of budding legal minds. These discussions are not just conversations; they're incubators for ideas, fostering a collaborative learning environment where every opinion adds a new dimension to your understanding.

articulate arguments effectively. This is where you learn to weave facts with legal principles, crafting compelling narratives that resonate with logic and empathy.

Embrace this journey of research and writing as a law student. It is here that you'll find your voice, develop your intellect, and prepare yourself for the impactful role you will play in the legal arena. Each paper you write is a step towards becoming not just a student of the law, but a master of its nuances and an advocate for its application.

Here are some of the reasons why writing research papers is important for law students:

- **Develop critical thinking skills:** Writing research papers requires law students to analyse, evaluate, and synthesize information from multiple sources. This process helps them develop critical thinking skills, which are essential for legal analysis and practice.

- **Improve legal research skills:** Law students must learn how to find and evaluate legal sources to support their arguments. Writing research papers can help them improve their legal research skills and learn how to use various legal databases, including LexisNexis and Westlaw.

- **Enhance writing skills:** Law students must write clearly and persuasively to communicate their arguments effectively. Writing research papers can help them hone their writing skills and learn how to write concisely and effectively. There is no hard and fast rule about the length of the research paper. The idea is to develop writing skills.

- **Format of research paper:** There is no set method for writing a good legal research paper. However, there are some basic qualities that establish a decent paper. Proper formation is one of the most important features necessary for you as a good writer. Even though a research paper in law has a specific nature, its general structure is confined to the introduction, main body, and conclusion. If making your paper's structure logical and concise is a tough task for you, look for help online.

- **Prepare for legal practice:** Many law students go on to practice law, where they will be required to write legal briefs, memos, and other documents. Writing research papers can help them develop the skills they need to succeed in legal practice.

- **Build a professional reputation:** Law students who write high-quality research papers may have the opportunity to present their work at legal conferences or submit their papers for publication. This can help them build a professional reputation and establish themselves as experts in a particular area of law.

Overall, writing research papers is an important aspect of the law school experience. It helps law students develop critical thinking, legal research, writing, and presentation skills, all of which are essential for success in legal practice.

- **Publishing Research Papers:** Law students can publish their research papers in a variety of venues, depending on their goals and the nature of their research. Here are some potential publishing options for law students:

- **Law Reviews:** Law reviews are academic journals that publish scholarly articles on legal topics. Many law schools have their own law reviews, and there are also many prestigious law reviews at other institutions. Publishing in a law review can be an excellent way for law students to showcase their research and establish themselves as experts in a particular area of law.

- **Student Journals:** Some law schools also have student-run journals that publish student-written articles. These journals may focus on a specific area of law or cover a broad range of legal topics.

- **Conferences:** Law students can also present their research at legal conferences, which can be an excellent way to get feedback on their work and network with other legal professionals.

- **Blogs (personal or public):** Some law students may choose to publish their research on legal blogs or websites. This can be a good option for students who want to reach a broader audience and get their work in front of practising attorneys or other legal professionals.

Law students can also use social media to promote their research and engage with others in the legal community. For example, they may share their research on Twitter or LinkedIn and engage in discussions with other legal professionals.

Overall, law students have many options for publishing their research papers, and the best option will depend on their goals and the nature of their research. It's important for law students to do their research and carefully consider which publishing options will best serve their needs.

3.11   Moot Courts should be made compulsory

Let's talk about moot courts — a must-do in your law school journey, especially here in India. So, why moot courts? They're like the gym for your legal muscles, giving you a real taste of courtroom battles. Mooting hones your skills in research, legal writing, and most importantly, oral arguments. You'll be tackling fictional cases, but the experience is incredibly real.

Now, what's in it for you? Apart from boosting your confidence and legal acumen, moot courts are a playground for critical thinking

I'm aware that moot courts aren't mandatory in Indian law schools, leading many students to bypass this opportunity. Unfortunately, it's often later in their careers that they recognize the missed value of participating in moot courts. This hesitation to engage often stems from a lack of confidence, an area where the support and guidance of the law school could make a significant difference. Effective handholding by the faculty can nurture students' confidence, encouraging them to take up moot court activities. I am of the strong view that certain number of moot courts should be make compulsory for every law student and should not be optional at all.

and public speaking. It's where theory meets practice, preparing you for the real legal world. And how do you ace them? By diving deep into your case, understanding every nook and cranny, and anticipating counter-arguments. It's all about strategy and presentation. This would not only enhance your legal skills but also prepare you for the practical challenges of the legal profession. It's vital for law schools to recognize this and actively foster an environment where every student feels empowered to participate in moot courts, understanding their immense long-term benefits.

Comparing this to international law firms, well, they highly value moot court experience. It shows you're not just book-smart but also courtroom-ready. Mooting reflects your ability to think on your feet and argue persuasively – skills that are gold in any legal setting, anywhere in the world. So, whether you're aiming for a career in India or dreaming of an international stage, moot courts are your stepping stone to greatness. Go for it and make every argument count!

But what about aspiring Corporate Lawyers? For them, moot courts can be tailored to focus on commercial and corporate law scenarios, like negotiating complex contracts and resolving corporate disputes. This approach bridges the gap between traditional moot court formats and the practical needs of corporate law practice. Such moot courts simulate real-world business environments, where students can engage in drafting, negotiating, and interpreting commercial agreements, mirroring the work they'll encounter in top-tier national and international law firms. This hands-on experience is invaluable, equipping future corporate lawyers with the skills needed to navigate the intricacies of the corporate legal world.

3.12   Innovative Initiatives beyond traditional Moot Courts

In recent years, global law schools have been exploring and adopting several innovative initiatives beyond traditional moot court competitions to provide practical training to students. Some of these initiatives include:

- **Legal Clinics:** Many law schools now offer legal clinics, where students work on real cases under the supervision of practicing attorneys. This hands-on experience can range from providing legal assistance to underserved communities to working on high-profile public interest cases.

- **Simulation Exercises**: Simulated negotiations, mediations, and trial advocacy exercises are becoming more common. These simulations often involve role-playing scenarios that mimic real-world legal situations, offering students a practical, immersive learning experience.

- **Externships and Fellowships**: Externships with law firms, courts, government agencies, and non-profit organizations offer on-the-job training. Fellowships might involve working on specific legal research projects or with advocacy groups, providing deeper insights into specialized legal fields.

- **Innovation and Technology Labs:** Some law schools have set up labs where students can work on legal technology and innovation projects, such as developing legal apps, exploring artificial intelligence in law, or working on access to justice technology projects.

- **Transactional Law Competitions:** For students interested in corporate law, transactional law competitions provide an opportunity to draft and negotiate business transactions, offering practical experience in a field where a traditional moot court may not.

- **Policy and Legislative Drafting Workshops:** These workshops allow students to work on drafting actual policy documents or legislation, giving them a taste of the legislative process and the intricacies involved in crafting legal texts.

- **International Arbitration Training:** With the rise in international trade and cross-border disputes, training in international arbitration, including participation in related competitions, provides valuable exposure to global legal practices.

- **Legal Hackathons and Design Thinking Workshops:** These events encourage students to use creative problem-solving skills to address legal challenges, often involving interdisciplinary collaboration.

- **Pro Bono Projects:** Engaging in pro bono work offers students the chance to work on real cases while serving the community, gaining practical experience and a sense of the societal role of legal professionals.

These initiatives reflect a growing recognition in legal education of the importance of practical, experiential learning. They aim to better equip law students with the skills needed to navigate the increasingly complex and dynamic legal landscape.

3.13 Pre-law classes: A great window to actionable insights

Even if you have decided to pursue a particular stream of law like Corporate, Securities, Banking, Constitutional, or Disputes, there is no harm in enrolling yourself for any undergraduate courses devoted to areas like Criminal Justice, Constitution, Environment, Political Science, Government, Economics, History, and Philosophy. Having a good grasp of a variety of topics is always useful in any practice area. Public speaking and debate courses are the best bet to boost your confidence as a law aspirant. Business courses devoted to Contract Law, Company Law, Securities Law, Banking and Finance, Foreign Collaborations, Mergers and Acquisitions, etc., will prove invaluable.

3.14 Soft Skills: the totally under-estimated competency

Whilst it is absolutely essential to gain a deeper understanding of the legal system – history, concepts, structures, functions, and terminology – it is equally important to work on your persona, passion, and values. There's a wealth of courses in the humanities and social sciences that will help sharpen your total personality including articulation, communication skills, and many others.

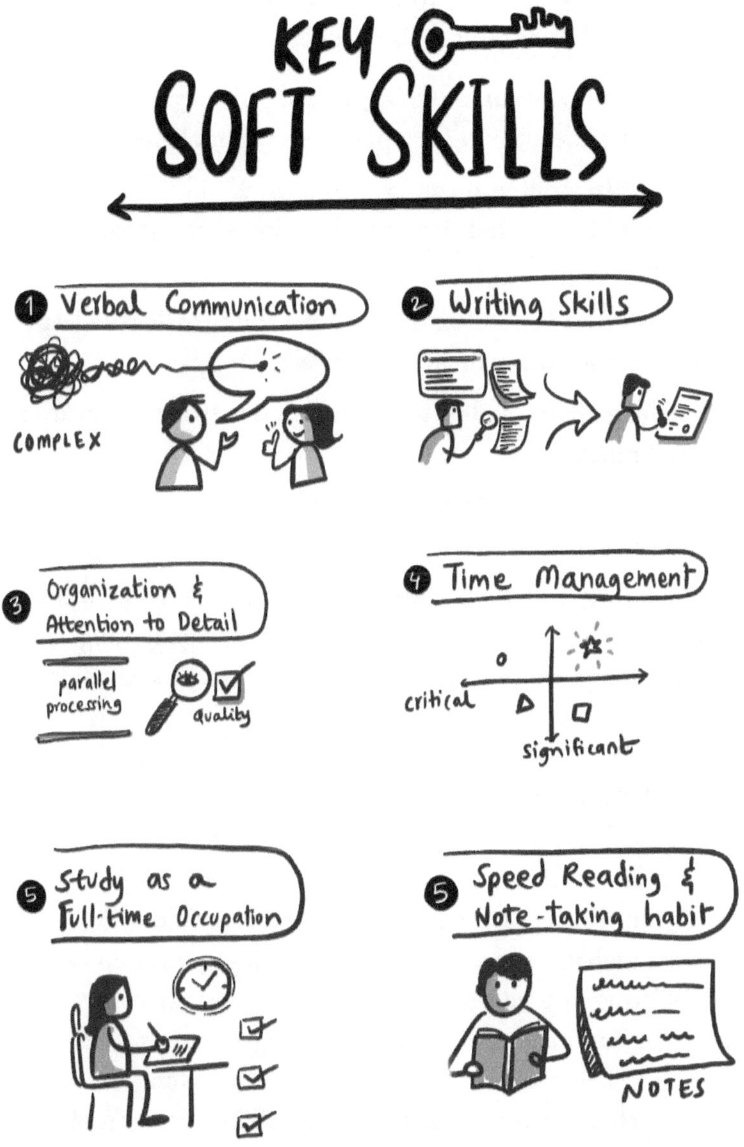

Proactively improve your soft skills (which includes undertaking scientific training by way of short courses (ideally offline) from any external agency/ faculty alongside law studies) like effective public speaking and writing as they hold the key towards building winning relationships with clients, superiors, subordinates, and other stakeholders. I would strongly urge Law Schools to take the lead and organise small awareness camps and also short courses on the law school campus itself; ideally, these courses should become an integral part of the curriculum. The key soft skills include:

- **Verbal communication**: the ability to demystify legal terms for non-legal parties, in short, explaining complex ideas in simple terms.

- **Writing skills:** Ability to collect, and analyze information, identify key issues, organise data, and draft a well-reasoned argument with a logical conclusion.

- **Organization and attention to detail:** the ability to do parallel processing and sharpen the quality of attention to all core areas.

- **Time management:** ability to prioritize tasks based on their criticality and significance.

- **Studying as a Full-Time Occupation:** Creating and scrupulously following a study schedule

- **Speed reading and note-taking habit**: creating notes through brisk reading sessions focused on identifying and highlighting key points; learning to outline and study the substantive and procedural law.

3.15 Core Skills and Experience

Entering the field of law is like setting out on a challenging yet rewarding journey. As a law student, it's essential to focus on certain core skills like problem-solving, writing and editing, and communication. Problem-solving is at the core of what lawyers do – it's about figuring out solutions to tricky situations. Writing and editing skills are crucial too, as clear and effective communication can make a big difference in legal matters. And speaking of communication, being able to talk and listen well is vital in understanding and addressing clients' needs. Remember, these skills are your tools for success in the legal world.

There is a plethora of self-help literature on the web as well as in print on essential skills and competencies which you can gainfully refer to and practice. Yet, I would like to stress upon the need to cultivate and sharpen the following core skills in particular, which go a long way in scripting a successful career in law.

- **Problem Solving-** analytical and problem-solving skills.

- **Critical Reading-** reading and critical analysis of complex textual material, judicial opinions, statutes, documents, and other written materials.

- **Writing and Editing-** practising rigorous and analytical writing, including preparing original pieces of substantial length and revising written work in response to constructive criticism.

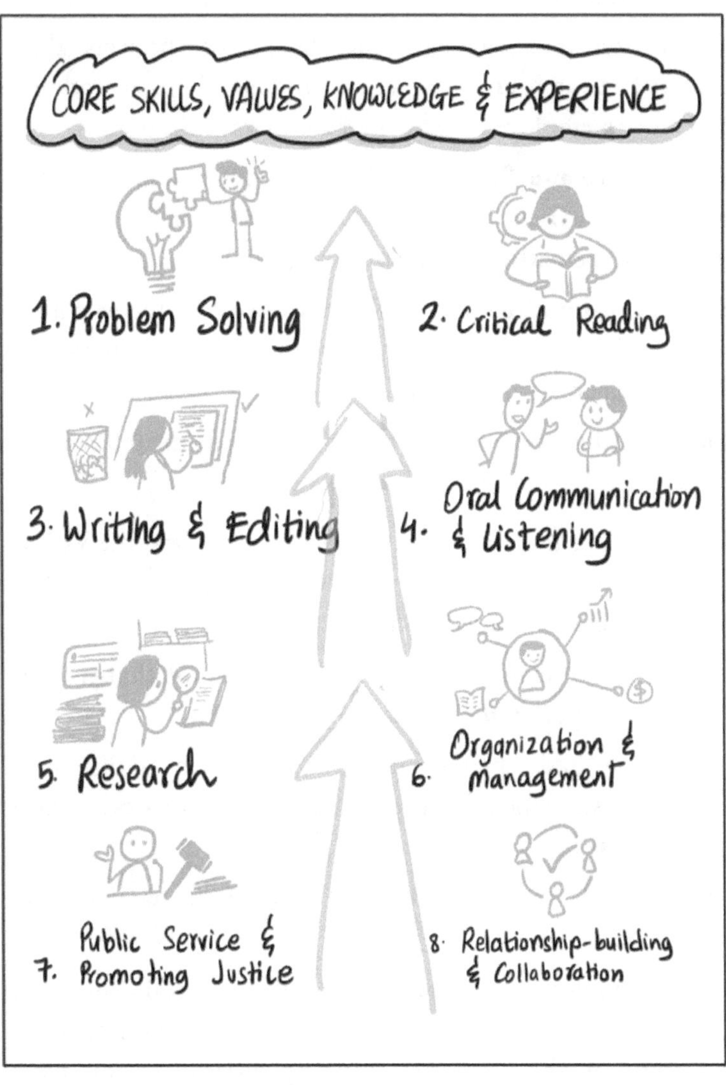

- **Oral Communication and Listening**- basic speaking and listening skills, such as engaging in debate, making formal presentations in class, or speaking before groups in school, the community, or the workplace.

- **Research**- experience in undertaking a project that requires significant library research and the analysis of large amounts of information obtained from that research.

- **Organization and Management**- taking on projects that require substantial research and writing, or through the preparation of major reports for an employer, a school, or a civic organization.

- **Public Service and Promoting Justice** - Participation in public service projects or similar efforts at achieving objectives established for common purposes can be particularly helpful.

- **Relationship-building and Collaboration**- Working as part of a team to build relationships for working with clients, co-counsel, opposing attorneys, expert witnesses, and others.

- **Fundamental Knowledge** – One should include the following into one's knowledge ammunition.

  - ✓ A broad understanding of history, including the various factors (social, political, economic, and cultural) that have influenced the development of our society.

  - ✓ A fundamental understanding of political thought and of the contemporary political system.

  - ✓ Some basic mathematical and financial skills, such as an understanding of basic pre-calculus mathematics and an ability to analyse financial data.

  - ✓ A basic understanding of human behaviour and social interaction.

  - ✓ An understanding of diverse cultures within and beyond the nation, of international institutions and issues, of world events, and of the increasing interdependence of the nations and communities within our world.

3.16   Follow SMART Mantra

To sum up I urge all law students to follow the SMART mantra for acquiring critical knowledge and experience from a practical lawyering perspective:

S - Skills Mastery and Assessment in Real-world Training: This component emphasizes the importance of developing practical skills and gaining hands-on experience through training programs that simulate real-world legal transactions. It also emphasizes the need for regular assessments to measure progress and identify areas for improvement.

M - Mentorship and Networking for Career Advancement: This component emphasizes the importance of mentorship and networking for career advancement in the legal profession. It encourages students to seek out mentors who can offer guidance and advice on navigating the legal profession and building a successful career.

A - Application of Legal Knowledge in Real-world Transactions: This component focuses on applying legal knowledge to real-world transactions and situations. It emphasizes the importance of understanding the practical implications of legal principles and developing actionable skills for effective legal practice.

R - Research and Analysis Techniques for Practical Legal Work: This component emphasizes the importance of research and analysis techniques for practical legal work. It encourages students to develop strong research and analytical skills to better understand complex legal issues and make sound legal decisions.

T - Technology Tools and Trends for Modern Legal Practice: This component focuses on the latest technology tools and trends that are transforming the legal profession. It encourages students to stay up-to-date with emerging technologies and use them to improve legal practice and provide better services to clients.

To reiterate, SMART for law students is designed to provide students with the requisite skills, knowledge, and experience they need to excel in the legal profession and become successful practitioners.

Chapter 4

Entry Into the Legal Profession

Entry into the legal profession in India has become increasingly difficult in the wake of the pandemic crisis, compounded by a clear oversupply of law graduates in the Indian legal market. The shift to virtual internships and the disruption of traditional recruitment processes have significantly limited hands-on experience and networking opportunities for aspiring lawyers. This saturation in the number of law graduates exacerbates the competition, demanding not just academic excellence but also the ability to adeptly navigate the new virtual landscape of the legal industry. Today's legal aspirants must be resilient and adaptable, embracing proactive learning and networking strategies to stand out in a market that is more challenging than ever.

Also, if one looks at the landscape of law firms in India which is markedly different from their counterparts in Europe or the United States, with a significant number being family-owned practices or smaller firms. This structure inherently limits their capacity to recruit in large numbers, unlike the larger international firms that often have extensive recruitment

Its high time that young lawyers adventure into setting up their own small boutique law firms and by adopting best practices and values growing them into full-fledged law firms of global size and significance.

programs. Consequently, the opportunities available for fresh law graduates in India are relatively fewer, intensifying competition in the job market.

The journey from law school to internship is an exciting phase of learning marked by energy and enthusiasm whereas the voyage from Internship to Trainee Associate is essentially a phase of discovery, and hence, often marked by more anxiety and constant stress. Things are worse for those who do not get placed in any law firm, lack industry experience, or do not get the opportunity to work with a senior lawyer. The competition is fierce, and I would recommend law students to ideally start working on getting placement from the third year onwards.

I know it can be a tremendous struggle for first-generation lawyers, particularly those coming from two or three-tier cities where there are not too many opportunities to earn and grow a decent practice. This, I guess, is the struggle faced not just by lawyers, but also by budding Chartered Accountants, Architects, Engineers, and other Consultants. So, what's the road to success?

Given the aforementioned, firstly, I would think it is important for you to start earning from the early days to support your dream and be a little financially independent. There are literally hundreds of options in today's age of information technology to earn. If you cannot find support for your own career, no one else can. Period. I started earning from my eighth standard by teaching Maths & Science to students of V to VIII, and I continued until I completed my law graduation (Please note there was no mobile, no internet or credit card in the 80s or early 90s). I was earning around Rs. 800 in 1980 as a tuition teacher, and merely Rs. 500 in 1988 as a law intern from a reputed law firm in Mumbai for almost 3 years till I passed my Solicitor Exam in 1991. Recently, one of my interns in Mumbai worked part-time for an online learning web portal and made decent money to sustain in Mumbai. Now, please don't ask me what can one do today to make around 20,000 a month apart from taking tuition.

It would not be out of place to mention how legendary trial lawyer Ram Jethmalani worked during his early days. He had to borrow money to pay rent and buy food. To begin with, he worked tirelessly, taking on cases that others might have shied away from. In his early days, he pro-bono defended a poor farmer who was accused of stealing cattle; he fought for a group of hawkers selling fruits and vegetables and being harassed by the police; he defended an artist who was arrested for drawing political cartoons and many such cases before he became famous defending the Nanavati Murder case. He stood up for the voiceless, using his legal expertise to bring about positive change in society.

Success is never overnight; it's a result of hard work, dedication, and an unwavering belief in one's abilities. Ram Jethmalani's story teaches us that with persistence, resilience, and a passion for justice, we can overcome any obstacle and achieve greatness in our chosen fields! Don't worry if 'Plan A' fails; there are 25 more letters in the alphabet.

4.1   First Placement - Here is the suggested way forward.

Identify the practice area where you wish to work: The first action point in this direction is to identify your area of practice – this is an extremely critical step. For example, if you wish to become a Corporate Lawyer, there are three branches: Corporate, Finance, and Securities law. Spend some time to understand the scope of these branches of law and find out the area you are interested in. Speak to experts about it or do detailed online research. If you are not sure, there is nothing wrong with exploring all three and then deciding. However, please do your homework thoroughly. I repeat this is an extremely critical stage which will go a long way in deciding and defining your career. Similarly, if you wish to pursue Criminal, Constitutional or any other branch of law, please spend adequate time understanding the scope and the way forward.

I would urge Law Schools to the take lead and invite senior lawyers/judges to have structured open discourse with students to answer all their basic questions and help them make an informed decision. Such conversations should be institutionalized by the Law Schools during the entire year to help students choose the right way forward.

Even Students could take a lead and organise such career-oriented guidance or discourse.

Next is to identify a few law firms where you wish to get recruited (keep a minimum of 3 to 4 backup plans ready). Once you have zeroed in on the list of law firms, you need to identify the partner you wish to work with. Understand the individual profiles of the firms and the partners. There is nothing wrong in speaking to them in advance, but don't ask them basic questions which could easily be covered through research. **Your objective should be to seek 'meaningful guidance', not to showcase your ignorance or intelligence. Don't forget that the senior lawyers have also gone through this grind – so, they would instantly know where you come from.**

Appearing for the final interview or for that matter, any interview, is all about how well you have prepared yourself. Speaking for myself, I divide any interview at any level into three parts (a) qualification and personality (attitude), (b) technical skills (no compromise), and (c) candidate's future plans (open to discussion). I repeat, before appearing for any interview, you should do YOUR HOMEWORK (*emphasis supplied*) on the firm, and the partner who you would interact with. There is enough material available on the internet on how you should appear for an interview, and I do not wish to reinvent the wheel here.

4.2   Day one of your first placement

Congratulations! If you have cracked the placement in one go, and that too in a firm and partner of your choice; more importantly, also with a bumper package you wished! That's called a dream come true, a remarkable achievement. Now, if you didn't do your homework on your firm/partner before the interview, please do it now before joining in person. This would help you pick up pace and get going in your career right from the word go. Many firms do have an induction program, wherein they take you through the dos and don'ts of the firm. Being enthusiastic and energetic is always good, but before you display your intellectual wares, I would strongly recommend that you invest enough time to understand and absorb the firm's culture, working pattern, people, and the like.

It is important to display the highest degree of ethics and discipline and stand out in the crowd. Be respectful and humble in your approach whilst dealing with people around you are, including your immediate senior/other seniors, colleagues, juniors, admin staff and clients. Don't forget all of them are equally important! Remember your competition is not and should not be with people around you. Your competition has to be with yourself.

As a fresh attorney (just passed), you are not expected to meet clients directly and deliver solutions from day one. You are expected to be a good listener and proactively follow instructions meticulously.

4.3   What if you are rejected?

"The real man smiles in trouble, gathers strength from distress, and grows brave by reflection." – Thomas Paine.

What if you don't make it? Firstly, don't be bitter or annoyed, and don't badmouth the firm or the partner who has interviewed you. Be calm – write down on a piece of paper where you think you missed or went wrong and try to improve next time. If possible, write a polite email (even if you are rejected) thanking the partner for his /her  **time and patience. Building bridges takes us further than building walls! Secondly, write a brief note on any aspect of yourself which you think you missed – period. For God's sake, don't try to teach any lesson or be arrogant in your response. Move ahead in life with renewed hope!**

You may have been destined to make a beginning somewhere with someone else. So, go back to your plan B and C and see what's best you can do. If none of your backup plans work, one option is to go back to these firms and seek an internship for some time (this is my personal view) because you need to remain engaged so that you can move ahead. Forget thinking about why you were rejected; find your own niche of specialization and pursue it vigorously, may take any additional diploma or certificate course so that you keep gaining specialized knowledge, and write more focused research papers, and blogs; if time permits invest your time in learning leadership skills like public speaking, writing, negotiations, team building. Stay in touch with your close friends, and also make new ones and keep learning. I am sure your work will be noticed sooner or later. **Remember, you will always get what you deserve, not necessarily what you desire or dream!**

4.4   Reputation as a lawyer

I would urge you all to consciously work and first try to be legally correct. **Go deep into the subject and try to avoid making any 'error' in law because you must build your reputation as a 'technically perfect'**

The more you work, the more you are going to learn; the more you learn the more you would be able to deliver; the more you deliver, the more your seniors/ colleagues would be dependent on you, and the more you would be in demand. That's the first step towards success!

lawyer. That's your first identity! Keep checking your thought process or interpretation with your colleagues or seniors and always put your best foot forward. There is no harm in you going and seeking time from your seniors or colleagues to discuss even simple interpretations. Spend two to three years being technically perfect in whatever you do. Don't shy away from or be lethargic in shouldering responsibilities.

Drafting precise legal documents requires careful attention to detail and thorough verification of terms.

Here's a suggestion for how you could draft a lesson from this experience: Once, I assigned a junior lawyer the task of defining the term 'affiliate' for a shareholders' agreement. He submitted a definition that referenced the term as defined in the Companies Act of 1956. Upon inquiry, I asked the junior lawyer if he had verified the definition from the Companies Act. He confidently affirmed that he had. However, when requested to show the reference, he struggled and ultimately, failed to locate it. This was not surprising, as the term 'affiliate' is not defined in the Companies Act of 1956. Realizing his mistake, he admitted to relying on his memory rather than rechecking the source.

I advised him that, even if one believes to have read or known a particular provision, it is critical to recheck the source before incorporating it into any legal document. This practice ensures accuracy and reliability in legal drafting.

Personal Experience: I shared with him my own practice of re-reading Section 340 in conjunction with Schedule XIII of the Companies Act, 1956 regarding Managerial Remuneration each time I issued an opinion on the matter. This was during the 90s when managerial remuneration was highly regulated for public companies and almost every company used to seek our advice on structuring the remuneration. Despite my familiarity with these sections, I made it a point to review them again for every new case or opinion. And this I do it till date. The reputation I gained with my seniors and clients was that I would never write any interpretation unless I checked the legal provisions thoroughly.

The essence of precise legal drafting lies in the meticulous verification of facts and laws. Assumptions or memory-based drafting can lead to inaccuracies and legal flaws. Therefore, it is paramount for legal professionals to consistently refer back to the original sources, ensuring that every piece of information used in legal documents is current, accurate, and thoroughly vetted. **This approach is fundamental to achieving a reputation of being legally perfect over a period of time.**

4.5   Associate to Mid-Level Attorney

As soon as you complete say 3 to 4 years as an associate, you would seek promotion and you may even get anxious about it, and I can totally understand that emotion. However, unfortunately, not many law firms have a clear path for promotion or even a scientific way of evaluating their associates. It's more based on their perception of you. However, I must say times are changing, and even smaller law firms are now trying to create merit-based organisations. Here, I may add that it is better to first do a self-assessment and try to be as objective as possible and evaluate the results. I have also noticed somehow young lawyers somehow feel restless in one firm after spending an initial 2 to 3 years. They just want change for the sake of changing. Also, by that time the learning curve slows down and they are overanxious to do challenging work. And when they see their peers in other firms do good work or earn a little more, they feel they are lagging behind. This is a dangerous zone! My simple advice here would be to be objective and not emotional in getting your facts right. Your competition should be with yourself!

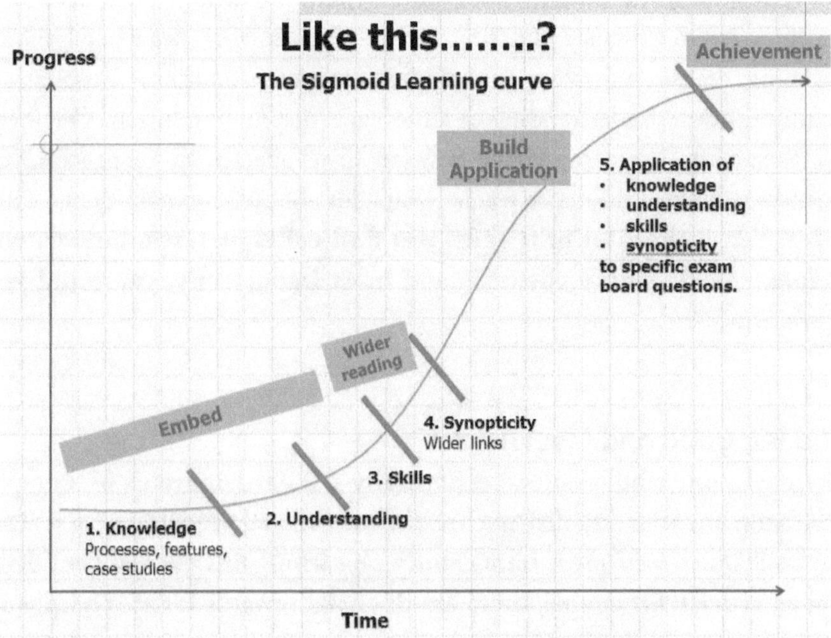

As one moves from an Associate to a Mid-level Attorney position, the situation demands that one should experiment a lot, and build confidence while aspiring to settle into a stable career over the long term. In law, one needs to swim with the tide. If one has done well in the initial phases, settling down as a mid-level attorney becomes comparatively easier.

The Sigmoid learning curve, resembling an "S" shape, illustrates the progression of learning over time. It starts with a slow initial phase, where learners grapple with basics. As understanding deepens, learning accelerates rapidly, marking the curve's steep middle section. This phase reflects quick gains in knowledge or skill. Eventually, the curve plateaus, indicating a slowing of learning as one approaches mastery. The curve encapsulates the journey from novice to expert, with varying learning intensities.

Learning during the initial phase includes a vast ocean. One needs to build a strong foundation in basic law, research abilities, drafting, writing, and communication skills to also keep pace with the fast-evolving legal developments. The learning curve is very steep as the practical aspect of law is not embedded in the law school curriculum. As a result, one gets the illusion of having learnt a lot if one does not proactively amass practical knowledge. In the whole effort to understand and grasp the rudiments of law theory, the aspects of practice can't be ignored.

The key is to do a lot of reading and interaction with real-world practitioners to enhance the skills of problem-solving, legal analysis and reasoning, legal research, factual investigation, drafting, negotiations, communication, understanding of issues, and dispute resolution. One needs to make an effort to comprehend how law firms operate. In the process, your expanding circle of influence teaches you a lot about the dynamics of a career in law. **You make a lot of friends, you find colleagues, you interact with seniors, you develop a clientele, and most importantly, you build your reputation.**

Who is a Good mid-level lawyer?

Obviously, one who is able to execute any standard or even a bit complex mandates; one who establishes a healthy working relationship with seniors, and colleagues, and most importantly one who gains clients' confidence is most crucial! Of course, there are financial rewards for this hard work

in the form of yearly increments, bonuses or incentive payments as per the policy of the law firm you work for.

In my opinion, as a Mid-level Lawyer, you must strive to build your overall reputation of being an excellent lawyer in, (1) sound legal interpretation, (2) wide-ranging research capabilities, (3) good drafting and negotiations skills, (4) excellent time management and teamwork and most importantly, (5) strong client handling and servicing. Trust me if you are sincere in these 5 aspects of practice, you will be able to generate independent business at your individual level. You will perform high-quality legal work, not only

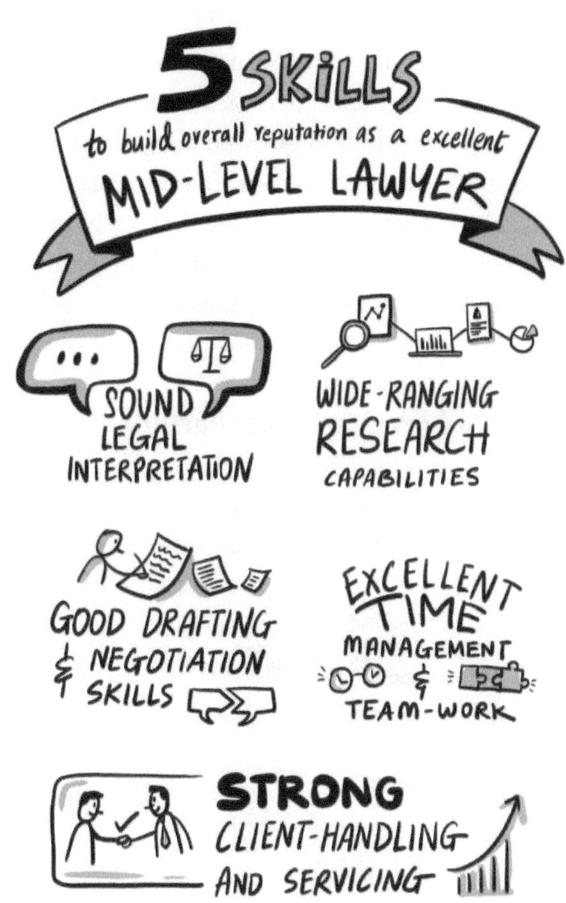

getting things right but also communicating "solutions" to clients in a way that it inspires confidence. You will do a good job at tracking new business opportunities from networking connections or events. Over time, you will develop your own leadership style and skills which, in turn, will enhance the reputation that you have already gained. **Most importantly, throughout your tenure, you should focus on the big picture of the firm if you wish to progress further in your law firm. Be proactive in critical areas like Knowledge Management, Information Technology, and Human Resource initiatives that will improve your individual brand visibility.**

In good time, you should be able to demonstrate value addition in your work matters; however, if you wish to move up the value chain, you must independently strive to identify a **new field of work** which will help you recognize and develop new clients on the sheer strength of your ability to provide solutions. As regards career progression, you need to study your firm's policies and find out whether there is any structured way of conducting assessments and promotions. If yes, is the process fair and impartial and are you able to discuss your way forward freely and without undue stress? In short, you need to assess whether the firm is investing in your training and grooming and candidly do your self-evaluation.

4.6 Mid-level to Equity Partner

Here, I would like to begin by saying that becoming an 'equity partner' of any top law firm is not an end in itself. **The central question is: are you viewed as the 'go-to lawyer' in your chosen area of practice?** Moving from Senior Associate to Equity Partner in a law firm is a significant career milestone that requires a combination of high-quality legal skills, good business acumen, and strong relationship-building abilities. Successful candidates must be able to demonstrate a track record of achievement in these areas and be committed to **providing high-quality legal services to clients while driving the firm's overall growth and success.**

Your role and responsibility as an intern

in any law firm versus an associate versus as a senior associate, followed by retained partner and finally equity partner are totally different. At the final stage, the technical capability to handle complex matters in your chosen area of practice is an absolute must! In fact, you are expected to be a thought leader who is recognized as an **authority** in your chosen practice area, capable of providing **innovative** and **forward-thinking solutions** to legal challenges. As a thought leader, are you able to **anticipate emerging trends** and **developments** and offer **strategic advice** and guidance to clients based on your knowledge and experience? You should be recognised as an **industry expert** leading discussions at various forums; this experience will help you articulate your **independent thoughts**. From any law firm's perspective, being a thought leader in your practice area as a lawyer means that you are seen as **a trusted advisor** and a valuable resource for clients and other professionals in your field.

To sum up in order to move up the value chain, you need to build and work around the five components, namely; (1) niche practice and thought leadership, (2) unique leadership style, (3) core network of people including seniors, colleagues, clients, friends, and prominent industry experts, (4) upgradation of technical and non-technical skills, and (5) a reputation that reflects your personality in terms of extra-ordinary listener, great communicator, keen to learn new things including technology, adept at meaningfully connecting with people, good team player, and demonstrating excellent work ethics, discipline, and time management.

Currently, the new trending areas of work are emerging technologies like AI, Robots, Data Analytics, IoT, Blockchain, Cloud Computing, emerging businesses like Online Retail (E-Commerce), Online Education (Edu-Tech), Healthcare (Med-Tech), Gaming, Financial Services (Fin-Tech),

Law schools play a crucial role in shaping the future of the legal profession, and it's essential for them to establish programs that consistently expose students to new industry domains. By engaging industry experts, academics, and thought leaders, these programs can offer a rich, multi-faceted learning experience. Regular interactions with professionals from various fields not only broadens the students' understanding of the legal landscape but also keeps them abreast of emerging trends and challenges. It's imperative for law schools to recognize this need and proactively create opportunities that nurture their students' development into well-rounded, informed legal professionals.

Agri-Tech, Food-Tech, Gig economy, and <u>emerging areas</u> like Alternate Dispute Resolution (ADRs), International Arbitrations, and Environmental, Social, and Corporate Governance (ESG.) Each of these areas is vast and would only get more complex and bigger. In each of these areas, do extensive research and comparative analysis, identify the commercial opportunity, track new developments, start connecting with/following the right people, create your thought leadership by writing blogs/articles and meaningful observations, take up speaking engagements, and be consistent in your efforts.

4.7   What if you don't make it as an Equity Partner?

Even after having worked hard for 10 to 12 years or even 15 years, don't get dejected if you are not made an Equity Partner because of whatever reasons (which may or may not be fully within your control). **Just because you don't make it, it doesn't mean you are not capable.**

There are multiple factors which are considered by firms, but key among them are, (a) first and foremost, whether you are capable of bringing new business (revenue) for the firm on your own, (b) secondly, whether you credibly reflect the firm's culture and values through your thoughts and actions, and (c) thirdly, are you a team player.

Note of caution – Many firms claim they prioritize skilful execution over new business acquisition, suggesting they mainly seek competent hands for their work. However, this perspective is often short-lived and misleading. It's a comforting notion, given that lawyers typically struggle with marketing their services. Yet, regardless of size, every firm ultimately expects its members to contribute by bringing in independent business. Your credibility in the firm would increase only if you were able to bring your own book of business. Period.

Becoming an equity partner also depends on whether your law firm (big or small) has a system of making process-driven promotions in a transparent, well-structured, and unbiased manner (which, unfortunately, is not the case still with many Indian law firms). I would suggest that in the initial 5 to 6 years if you realize that the firm lacks a 'structured process' or objective evaluation for promotion, you should look out for a change. You cannot grow at the mercy of one or two individuals. Here, I would strongly recommend joining an even smaller

boutique law firm where growth is certain and opportunities abound, or you could simply start on your own, work hard and move up the value chain.

The expansion of any law firm is nothing but an increase in headcount. People are the plant and machinery of any consultancy firm, including law firms and the majority of them stagnate or struggle to grow because they are unable to recruit more and more competent people. More people mean different working patterns, diverse cultures, varied thoughts, and independent behaviours. The leadership of any law firm, in my reckoning, must be democratic and not authoritative. The key questions are: does the firm care for and value people? Have you tried to build a good working relationship and rapport with others in the organization? Unfortunately, people are knowingly or unknowingly in constant competition with their own colleagues, and that's fatal. **Remember our network is our net worth**!

I would like to share the conversation with my professor when I signed up for my Solicitors Exam in 1988 (exactly 32 years back!) I asked him, "What if I don't pass the Solicitors Exam?" My Prof. replied, "First clear your exam, work hard and if you still don't succeed, then we will see." I was confused and more upset. But I was determined to clear my Solicitors Exam first, and then, think what next. I am glad I heeded my professor's advice.

I guess this futuristic question is faced by almost every ambitious young boy or girl from any field. I can only ask them to internalize what Steve Jobs said at Stanford -

"You can't connect the dots looking forward; you can only connect them looking backwards. So, you have to trust that the dots will somehow connect in your future. You have to trust in something – your gut, destiny, life, karma, whatever. Because believing that the dots will connect down the road will give you the confidence to follow your heart even when it leads you off the well-worn path, and that will make all the difference."

I can only say that have the courage to follow your heart.

4.8   Achieving Success as an Equity Partner

To sum up, SUCCESS in terms of an Equity Partner whether in a large law firm or any boutique small firm would mean:

S - Strong Work Ethic and Professionalism: This component emphasizes the importance of a strong work ethic, professional conduct, and adherence to ethical standards in the legal profession.

U - Understanding of Firm Culture and Dynamics: This component focuses on understanding the culture and dynamics of the law firm where the graduate is employed. It encourages graduates to adapt to the firm's work style, policies, and procedures to fit in seamlessly.

C - Competence in Legal Research and Problem-Solving Skills: This component focuses on the importance of developing legal research, analysis and problem-solving skills.

C - Client Management Skills: This component emphasizes the importance of your ability to manage clients effectively establish trust and rapport and manage client expectations effectively.

E - Efficient Problem-Solving Skills: This component emphasizes the importance of efficient problem-solving skills. The need to identify potential problems early and find creative solutions to resolve them amicably satisfactory to client needs.

S - Strong Interpersonal Skills and Teamwork Abilities: This component focuses on the importance of strong interpersonal skills and teamwork abilities. It encourages you to work collaboratively with colleagues, build effective relationships, and resolve conflicts constructively.

S - Striving for Continuous Learning and Professional Development: This component emphasizes the importance of continuous learning and professional development in the legal profession. It encourages us to stay updated with the latest at all times.

4.9 Becoming a Corporate Lawyer

Becoming a corporate lawyer in India has become a new craze, if I may say so; but few realize that is a challenging journey, and it requires focused effort and dedication. The liberalization of Foreign Direct Investment (FDI) in India in 1991 led to a significant increase in foreign investment and business activities in India. Joint Ventures and Foreign Collaborations were the order of the day. Every large foreign company wanted to be in India and the best alternative was to be in a JV with a local partner. This resulted in a higher demand for specialised legal services which created a new breed of 'business/corporate lawyers or transactional lawyers.' The liberalisation of FDI also opened up several sectors such as telecom, banking, insurance, infrastructure, and manufacturing, which created more opportunities for corporate lawyers to work on complex and high-value transactions and partnerships.

Corporate lawyers were needed to advise foreign investors on the legal framework of doing business in India, including the regulatory and compliance requirements. They were also required to assist in negotiating and drafting agreements, resolving disputes, and handling mergers and acquisitions. More importantly, Indian lawyers started working with and in fact, travelling abroad to interact with International law firms who represented foreign companies; similarly, international law firms started visiting India on a regular basis.

International law firms brought with them new legal concepts, practices, and methodologies, which Indian lawyers began to incorporate into their legal practices. They learned about international best practices, advanced legal research techniques, and the use of technology to manage global transactions more efficiently. This led to a significant improvement in the quality of legal services offered in India.

In addition, the age of information technology has made it easier for Indian lawyers to learn from their international counterparts. Online legal resources and research tools have made it possible for Indian lawyers to access legal information and research from around the world. They can stay up to date with the latest legal developments and best practices, allowing them to provide high-quality legal services to their clients.

Earlier, SEBI was established in 1992, which introduced several new legislations to deal with listed and unlisted securities, like the SEBI Takeover Code, Insider Regulations, Issue of Capital and Disclosures, and a plethora of guidelines related to securities like the FII investment; FERA was replaced by FEMA in 1999; followed by Competition Act, 2002 (repealing the Monopolies and Restrictive Trade Practices Act, 1969).and finally, the new Companies Act, 2013.

Furthermore, the emergence of international arbitration has also provided opportunities for Indian lawyers to work with international lawyers and learn from them. The rise of cross-border disputes has led to an increase in the use of international arbitration as a means of resolving disputes. This has provided opportunities for Indian lawyers to work with international lawyers and learn about international dispute resolution mechanisms and practices.

Thus, the liberalisation of the Indian economy since 1991 and the age of information technology provided Indian lawyers with opportunities to learn from their international counterparts. This has resulted in an improvement in the quality of legal services offered in India and has allowed Indian lawyers to compete at a global level.

Now, with the advent of generative AI, corporate lawyers stand to benefit significantly from enhanced efficiency and accuracy in their work. AI tools can swiftly draft and review complex legal documents, ensuring compliance with current laws and regulations while reducing the potential for human error. They also offer predictive analytics for better decision-making, automate routine tasks, and personalize client interactions, freeing lawyers to focus on more strategic, high-value aspects of their practice. This technological advancement not only streamlines workflow but also enhances the overall quality of legal services, allowing corporate lawyers to meet the evolving demands of their profession with greater agility and precision.

I consider myself and other lawyers who passed during the 1990s and got the opportunity to work on foreign collaborations as 'blessed' because we got to learn the entire spectrum of corporate laws slowly and in steps. Speaking for myself after becoming a Solicitor in May 1991, I got an opportunity to work with Mr. R. A. Shah (Sr. Partner of Crawford Bayley & Co.) one of the oldest law firms in India. Mr. Shah was an independent director/ vice chairman of many multinational companies like Colgate, BASF, Abbott, etc. He worked for many MNCs to raise their equity and/or form joint ventures wherein I got to learn closely from him and also from international lawyers and general counsel – see my journey as a Corporate lawyer in the last chapter.

Typically, Corporate Advisory inlcudes, A. Transactional, B. Opinions and C. Corporate Advisory..

A. Transactional Work

Often students and young lawyers ask me, to guide on simple workflow that he / sher should follow on any transaction (start to finish) be it any M&A or Private Equity or Setting up of a Joint Venture, without any mistake.

Every law firm and senior lawyer has their own unique way of handling transactions, from drafting term sheets to the grand closing. The key, in my view, lies in simplicity and staying laser-focused on the essentials. So, here's my method:

(i) First things first, your priority should be to understand exactly what the client aims to achieve in the proposed transaction. More importantly commercially what the client is expecting out of the deal and if possible, improve upon the same; Unfortunately, too not many lawyers even get to the real commercial angle quickly.

(ii) Next up, I dive headfirst into the complete regulatory landscape. The key approvals or permissions required and the process to obtain those including regulatory filings, if any. No stone is left unturned here because compliance is non-negotiable.

(iii) Finally, I meticulously outline all the documents required to structure the transaction and the key covenants of such documents.

Now, here's the twist – prepare a simple, informal memo or checklist to capture the aforesaid. No fancy format, just bullet points capturing these three crucial aspects: client's goals, regulatory requirements, and necessary documentation. Remember this is an internal guide and not for circulation to the others side because this is tailored for your client's requirements!

Update this checklist regularly and discuss it with clients so that there are no surprises at the last moment! But here's the real kicker – I keep an eagle eye on regulatory compliance & timelines throughout the process and more particularly during the closing. Missing a compliance detail is a no-go zone.

This informal memo / checklist serves as my trusted companion throughout the transaction. It would keep you on track, ensuring that you don't miss a beat. It's the simplest way to navigate complex transactions without stress.

B. Opinion Work

A lawyer's reputation hinges on their clarity of thought and firmness of advice. Thus, thorough analysis of the facts and relevant laws is paramount in preparing an opinion. A good opinion maker possesses several key qualities:

- **Analytical Skills:** The ability to dissect complex issues, identify essential details, and draw logical conclusions is essential.

- **Legal Knowledge:** A strong understanding of the law, regulations, and precedents relevant to the issue at hand is crucial.

- **Communication Skills:** Clear and concise communication ensures that the opinion is easily understood by the client and other stakeholders.

- **Objectivity:** Remaining impartial and objective in assessing the facts and providing advice is vital for credibility.

By honing these qualities and diligently applying them to each opinion, a lawyer can establish themselves as a trusted advisor, known for their clarity of thinking and sound judgment.

Here's a simple guide to preparing an Opinion:

- **Identify the Issue:** Start by clearly understanding the exact issue at hand. What question or problem needs addressing? What is the purpose of your opinion? For this careful listening to clients is extremely important. Today I see lots of clients are informed and well-read. Do not make the mistake of underestimating anyone. Time spent to understand the issue is time well spent. The Golden Rule of opinion writing is don't jump to conclusion in first meeting.

- **Client Perspective**: Consider the client's perspective and objectives. What outcome are they seeking? Understanding their needs is crucial. As I said please do not jump to a conclusion in the first meeting itself.

- **Thorough Analysis**: Conduct a comprehensive analysis of the relevant facts, laws, regulations, and precedents related to the issue. Find out if there are case laws identical to the facts at hand or supporting your views, this would give you lot of confidence and credibility to your opinion.

- **Outcome Clarity**: Your opinion may lead to three possible outcomes: a clear positive answer, a clear negative answer, or a gray area where the answer isn't straightforward. Once you have clarity of thoughts, please discuss the same with clients, before you start writing the final opinion. It is possible that new issues may come up, which you will have to deal with.

- **Draft Clear and in Simple Language**: Communication is key. Write your opinion in simple, clear language that is easy for the client to understand. I have seen opinions that run into several number of pages and are so complex that one may need another opinion to interpret such opinions. I have also seen opinions that are full of disclaimers and finally the real opinion could be in one last line.

- **Address the Exact Issue**: Focus your opinion directly on the issue at hand. Avoid unnecessary information or tangents. I would highly recommend extensive reading of Supreme Court decisions where you may get to read alternative views and the way it goes to the bottom of the issue involved. It is also important to read and understand laws of interpretation.

Remember, writing an opinion is a skill that improves with practice. Keep refining your approach to provide valuable and insightful guidance to your clients.

C. Corporate Advisory

This includes, on the one hand providing strategic advice to businesses on legal matters related to their operations, transactions and on the other incorporating a company, setting up partnerships or LLPs to secretarial compliances including advising on corporate governance and ESG compliances. To excel in this field, one must go beyond mere compliance and strive to become a trusted advisor to clients.

A good corporate advisor is someone who can anticipate their client's needs, offer creative solutions to complex problems, and communicate effectively with stakeholders at all levels of the organization. In order to be a specialist corporate lawyer, one would need to have specific industry knowledge.

How to get any specific Industry Knowledge:
I often find young lawyers struggle to get hang of any specific industry like Banking, Insurance, Manufacturing, Automobile, Telecom, Retail, Pharma, Infrastructure, IT, EdTech, FinTech,

First things first, let's break it down into three essential components:

1. The Business Model: What makes the business tick?
2. The Regulatory Regime: What rules and regulations govern its operations?
3. The Risks Factors and Management perception: What challenges does it face? and how the management deals with the same. This is the crux!

Please check if the company you're interested in is listed. If it is, go to their website or the Bombay Stock Exchange Limited (BSE) website. Find their last Prospectus, even if it's a little older, it's still gold. The prospectus is where the business model is laid out in complete details with critical contracts & collaborations. It also dives deep into the regulatory regime, outlining the permissions & approvals they adhere to. Most importantly, it highlights the risk factors with a detailed analysis and management perception. Read each part very carefully.

No matter even if you're not a securities lawyer. This document is your only one stop gateway to understand that business. To level up, study prospectuses of companies in similar industries – for e.g., banking, pharma, infrastructure, chemicals, IT, you name it!

But the golden rule is don't rush. Take your time, understand, analyse, and study carefully. Get a firm grip on one industry before diving into others.

Don't forget to stay updated with news related to that industry from business newspapers. In my opinion this is the only the best way to master any industry domain.

Like Moot Courts, Law Schools could consider organizing discussions on Industry specialization.

Young lawyers wanting to join corporate as inchouse counsel or general counsel should study that industry in detail before going for any interview and see the difference!

Getting good mentor and healthy working culture:
Typically associates find it difficult to find a good mentor or a good healthy working culture and are unable to focus on work in any toxic work environment. It's a challenge many of us have faced, and this could be at any stage of your career. Many associates find it difficult to navigate or find an alternate. In such situations here is my take:

First things first; there's no such thing as an "ideal" team or work environment, especially in the competitive world we navigate. Whether you're in law, accounting, engineering, or any other field, every team has its quirks and dynamics.

In the early days, 'patience' is the only your greatest ally! Refocus on learning, absorbing knowledge, and developing new skills. I don't find people investing quality time in learning skills. The moment you feel you're no longer learning in one place; it might be time to explore new horizons.

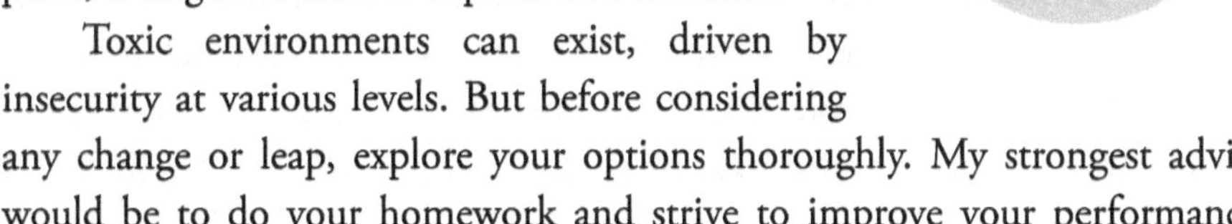

Toxic environments can exist, driven by insecurity at various levels. But before considering any change or leap, explore your options thoroughly. My strongest advice would be to do your homework and strive to improve your performance. Remember, your toxic team members are not your permanent colleagues.

When you consistently deliver exceptional work without showing you are disturbed, your colleagues and seniors will automatically change. Don't worry. Your mentors can be partners or mid-level professionals; what matters most is the mentor's ability to guide and support your growth. If he or she is not a good human being, it's time to simply change.

It's essential to maintain a growth mindset and focus on self-improvement. While challenges may arise, they also present opportunities for personal and professional development. Keep your eye on your goals, and success will follow! Trust me.

Remember, what brought you to this point won't necessarily take you further. Be adaptable, embrace change, and keep evolving in your career journey.

Challenges in Corporate Law Practice:

Today 'Corporate law and in particular M&A practice' is well established in India. However, here are some of the main challenges that aspiring corporate lawyers in India may face:

- **Tremendous Competition:** Corporate law is not just a popular but an extraordinarily competitive field in India. This is because a majority of law students and young lawyers vying for a limited number of positions. As a result, it can be challenging to stand out from the crowd and secure a good position in this field.

- **Rigorous and structured education and training:** Becoming a corporate lawyer requires not just a rigorous but an extremely structured education and practical training process, from the law school level itself, which, today, seems still absent in India. The real change in the landscape of corporate laws started in 1991 (see above) and any law student he/she has would have to do extensive reading of changes/introduction of new laws and regulations from FEMA/ SEBI/ Competition Law/IBC and allied laws to be able to even understand and appreciate mergers and acquisitions, divestitures and demergers, foreign investment and foreign collaborations, technology transfers, licensing of intellectual property rights, fundraising from angel investors to structuring private equity investments, conducting legal due diligence, preparing terms sheets to definitive documents and issuing closing opinions.

- **Demanding work environment:** Corporate lawyers work in a fast-paced and high-pressure environment, and they must be able to handle large volumes of work and meet tight deadlines. This can be challenging for new lawyers who are still learning the ropes and building their basic learning and practical skills.

- **Continuous learning and professional development:** Corporate law is a constantly evolving field, and lawyers must stay up to date with changes in the law and the regulatory regime literally on a daily basis. This requires continuous learning and professional development, which can be challenging for lawyers who are also managing a busy workload.

- **High expectations:** Clients and employers have high expectations for corporate lawyers, and they expect them to provide high-quality, practical, and timely legal advice. This can be challenging for new lawyers who are still building their experience and developing their legal skills.

Overall, becoming a corporate lawyer in India requires a combination of education, structured training, hard work, and perseverance. It's important for aspiring lawyers to be prepared for the challenges they may face and to remain committed to their career goals despite the obstacles that may arise.

Adopt the **three 'E' Formula** to become a successful corporate lawyer. The more you explore, the more you expand and express.

EXPLORE

Study the provisions of all applicable laws in relation to M&A including Companies Act, 2013, SEBI Takeover Regulations/FEMA/Competition Act, and allied Rules and Regulations. Prepare a detailed chart/notes on the legal process, key steps, legal Due-diligence and Documentation including

Term-Sheet, Various types of M&A Schemes including Demergers along with a detailed Timetable for implementing M&A (for both listed and unlisted companies). Make exhaustive personal notes and a rich repository of reference material.

Study major Court decisions dealing with various issues arising during M&A including valuation, the role of directors, dissenting and minority shareholders, creditors, employees, the applicability of competition law/exchange control regulations, public policy, industry-specific regulatory regime, common objections by regional directors, SEBI, Income Tax, and the like. Retain copies of important decisions with your own personal markings.

Study various models of JVs, documentation involved like Share Purchase Agreement, Share Subscription Agreement, Shareholders' Agreement or Joint Venture Agreement and other Ancillary Agreements such as Trademark License Agreement, Marketing and Distributorship Agreement, Export Promotion Agreement, Manufacturing Agreement (also called as Toll Manufacturing), Technology Transfer or License Agreement, Agreement to Depute Technicians, Employment Agreements, Agreement to Rent Office. Collect drafts of these documents and diligently practice drafting these agreements.

EXPAND

Develop a habit of reading key business newspapers and magazines to track business news in India and globally across industries and service sectors. Read various articles, reports, analyses, and research publications on M&A from leading consulting companies like McKinsey/Bain/international universities like Harvard/Oxford/London Business School/Forbes. Maintain newspaper cuttings/articles for future reference.

EXPRESS

Write columns, articles, or research papers on topics on interesting topics in newspapers or post them on your social media. Regularly attend seminars/discussions as an audience and seek speaker engagements on diverse subjects at your own law schools, Institute of Company Secretaries, Institute of Chartered Accountants and other key forums.

4.10 ESG and SDG - Next Big Buzzwords

Let's talk about two crucial concepts that are shaping the future of business and law: ESG and SDG. ESG, or Environmental, Social, and Governance, is a set of standards for a company's operations that socially conscious investors use to screen potential investments. It's like a report card showing how a company performs as a steward of nature, how it manages relationships with employees, suppliers, customers, and communities, and how it handles its leadership, audits, and internal controls.

Then, there's SDG or Sustainable Development Goals. These are 17 goals created by the United Nations to address global challenges like poverty, inequality, climate change, environmental degradation, peace, and justice. Think of them as a blueprint for peace and prosperity for people and the planet, now and into the future.

Understanding ESG and SDG is crucial for anyone stepping into the corporate world, especially for future lawyers. It's about aligning legal expertise with ethical and sustainable business practices. So, as we dive deeper, remember, it's not just about following laws; it's about leading the charge towards a better, more sustainable world.

Now, for law students who want to become great corporate lawyers, here's what you need to do:

- **Learn About ESG and SDG:** Start by understanding what ESG and SDG really mean and why they are important. Read up, take courses, or attend workshops to get a good grip on these topics.

- **Think Beyond Just Law:** As a future lawyer, remember it's not just about knowing the legal stuff. You need to understand how businesses impact the environment and society. So, broaden your knowledge about climate change, social justice, and ethical business practices.

- **Get Practical Experience:** Try to get internships or work on projects that involve ESG or SDG matters. This will give you real-world experience and show you how these concepts are applied in business.

- **Stay Updated:** These areas are always changing, so keep yourself updated with the latest developments in ESG and SDG. Follow the news, read articles, and join relevant groups or forums.

- **Bring ESG and SDG into Your Work:** Once you start working, always think about how your legal advice can help companies be better at ESG and SDG. It's about guiding them to not only follow the law but also do good for the world.

So, if you're keen on being a corporate lawyer, getting into ESG and SDG is a smart move. It's about helping businesses do well while also doing good for the planet and its people.

4.11   Encountering Hurdles and the Way Forward

"I can control my destiny, but not my fate. Destiny means there are opportunities to turn right or left, but fate is a one-way street. I believe we all have the choice as to whether we fulfil our destiny, but our fate is sealed."

- Paulo Coelho

It is possible that we don't get what we desperately yearned for! Often, our close relatives and friends don't support us when we expect them to stand firmly behind us. In short, things often don't fall in place as we think; on the contrary, we get exactly what we tried to avoid. We feel dejected and more frustrated because we don't find a quick solution. Every one of us would face this situation not just once but on many occasions in professional and personal life alike. Friends, there is no straight-jacket formula or a silver bullet solution to any of these situations. I can only share what I have been following and would like to reassure you that it has worked so far. By now, I guess you must be familiar with the legal terminologies. If you happen to go to court, you will notice that the most common order passed in the majority of the complex matters is called as 'status quo' order. Which means no change! **So, in difficult situations, the best decision is to 'maintain status quo' – No Change. No change until you identify and deal with the 'root cause' of the problem or situation.**

To find the root cause of any problem, there are multiple theories and techniques developed over a period of time. One such theory is "**The Five WHYs theory**". It is an iterative, interrogative technique used to explore the cause-and-effect relationships underlying a particular problem. The primary goal of the technique is to determine the root cause of a defect or problem by repeating the question 'Why?' five times. The answer to the fifth 'why' should reveal the root cause of the problem. The technique was described by Taiichi Ohno at Toyota Motor Corporation.

Example

Problem: The vehicle will not start.

Why? – Is the battery dead? The alternator is not functioning.
Why? – Is the alternator not functioning? The alternator belt is broken.
Why? – Is the alternator belt broken? It has exceeded its useful service life
Why? – Alternator belt exceed its useful life? It has not been replaced.
Why? – was the alternator belt not replaced? The recommended service schedule was not followed (root cause)

The questioning for this example could be taken further to a sixth, seventh, or higher level, but five iterations of asking why are generally sufficient to get to a root cause. The key is to encourage the troubleshooter to avoid assumptions and logic traps and instead trace the chain of causality in direct increments from the effect through layers of abstraction to a root cause that is connected to the original problem. In this example, the fifth "why" suggests a broken process or an alterable behaviour, which is indicative of reaching the root-cause level.

The last answer points to a process. This is one of the most important aspects of the Five Whys approach – the real root cause should point toward a process that is not working well or does not exist. Untrained facilitators will often observe that answers seem to point towards classical answers such as not enough time, not enough investments, or not enough resources. These answers may be true, but they are out of our control. Therefore, instead of asking why, **ask why the process failed.**

Now let's turn on some of the basic questions that any law student faces and find out the root cause and the probable answers following the Five Whys technique. The idea here is to develop a process to help you envision and find solutions to typical issues arising in the future.

4.12   CASE STUDY 1

Let's take an interesting example and see the Five Whys to identify possible reasons why you were not selected to work as an associate in a good, reputed law firm.

Why was I not selected to work as an associate in a good, reputed law firm?
Possible answer: Because I did not perform well during the interview process.

Why did I not perform well during the interview process?
Possible answer: Because I did not adequately prepare for the interview or research the firm beforehand.

Why did I not adequately prepare for the interview or research the firm beforehand?
Possible answer: Because I underestimated the importance of preparation or did not know how to effectively prepare for a law firm interview.

Why did I underestimate the importance of preparation or not know how to effectively prepare for a law firm interview?
Possible answer: Because I did not seek advice or guidance from mentors, professors, or career advisors.

Why did I not seek advice or guidance from mentors, professors, or career advisors?
Possible answer: Because I was overconfident in my abilities, did not value the importance of networking and seeking advice, or did not have access to the right resources.

These are just a few possible reasons why you may not have been selected to work as an associate in a good, reputed law firm. By asking "why" multiple times and digging deeper into the underlying factors contributing to the problem, you can gain a better understanding of the root causes and take steps to address them in future job search and interview processes.

4.13   CASE STUDY 2

Let's take another interesting example and see the five whys to identify possible reasons why you did not become a partner in a law firm.

Why did I not become a partner in a law firm?
Possible answer: Because I did not meet the required billable hours target.

Why did I not meet the required billable hours target?
Possible answer: Because I did not effectively manage my time and failed to prioritize my workload.

Why did I not effectively manage my time and fail to prioritize my workload?
Possible answer: Because I did not have a clear understanding of the firm's expectations or how to balance competing demands.

Why did I not have a clear understanding of the firm's expectations or how to balance competing demands?
Possible answer: Because I did not ask for guidance or seek feedback on my performance.

Why did I not ask for guidance or seek feedback on my performance?
Possible answer: Because I was not aware of the importance of seeking feedback in ensuring professional growth.

These are just a few possible reasons why you may not have become a partner in a law firm. By asking "why" multiple times and digging deeper into the underlying factors contributing to the problem, you can gain a better understanding of the root causes and take steps to address them.

4.14   CASE STUDY 3

Let's take one more interesting example and see the five whys to identify possible reasons why you were unable to be a successful lawyer.

Why am I unable to be a successful lawyer?
Possible answer: Because I am still not a good technical lawyer who can attract good clients.

Why am I not able to do technical work?
Possible answer: Because I am not properly trained and lack practical experience.

Why am I not properly trained and lack practical experience?
Possible answer: Because I did not communicate effectively with my colleagues and supervisors, or did not take on work that aligns with my skills and strengths.

Why am I not communicating effectively with my colleagues and supervisors, or did not take on work that aligns with my skills and strengths?
Possible answer: Because I am not receiving adequate feedback or guidance from my supervisors, or I was lethargic in my work and did not seek opportunities to develop my skills and knowledge.

Why am I not receiving adequate feedback or guidance from my supervisors, or seeking out opportunities to develop my skills and knowledge?
Possible answer: Because I am not proactive in moving up the value chain, or I am not advocating for myself and my professional development.

It is imperative that we work on finding the root cause of our failure or what possibly could have gone wrong in a more scientific way and find solutions. Most of the time we try to find fault with others (which may be right). However, it leads to us making emotional decisions which could be more fatal.

Chapter 5

Challenges

"If there were no bad people, there would be no good lawyers"

- Charles Dickens

To counter challenges in any sphere, it is elementary to accurately identify key questions before seeking credible answers. The field of law is no exception. Students of law face a host of sticky challenges in the course of their education, and the onus is on the government and the fraternity to delve deep into the root cause of the problem and arrive at feasible solutions. This collective effort is imperative if we are to create a robust pool of competent and conscientious lawyers of tomorrow.

In this section, let us take a closer look at the various challenges that come in the way of quality education in law, which call for major reforms aimed at closing down mediocre, dubious and substandard law colleges.

5.1 Perils of Privatisation.

The first and perhaps the darkest blot on the legal education system in India is the 'privatization of legal education,' which has seen a plethora of law colleges emerging across the country. As the quality of education has been unknowingly marred by the lopsided focus on numbers, this supply-side boom has diluted the Indian brand of legal education which is nowhere close to matching global benchmarks.

Today, many legal institutions are owned and operated by businessmen and property developers as they were quick to find a lucrative economic venture in this domain. Many universities are focused on maximising profits rather than raising the quality of legal education.

The academic standards of these subpar commercial endeavours have remained below par as reflected by the mediocre calibre of the staff and students and abysmally low weightage given to research and development. While a few private colleges offer good placements and internship opportunities, the majority of law students are left to fend for themselves by pursuing a career in law.

The sorry state of affairs can be gauged from the following hard facts:

(a) A look back in time helps put the problem in perspective. In 1958, India had 43 law institutions serving 20,159 students. The enactment of the Advocates Act, 1961 was a turning point in the volume game which triggered the growth of sub-standard law schools. Given that aspirants with low scores of even 35 to 40 per cent could secure admission to a law course, students who were denied admission in any other course would take up law by default. Most of these law schools largely recruited part-time law teachers and provided poor infrastructural facilities. Obviously, student absenteeism was high on campus and the quality of law graduates was below par. The Supreme Court rightly observed in the Unni Krishnan, J.P. v. State of A.P. case that "education cannot be allowed to be converted into commerce."

(b) This affiliated law college system of state institutions is the Achilles heel of legal education in India. Most law colleges have institutionalised mediocrity through a discernible lowering of academic standards. Too many ineffective attorneys have lowered the bar for both legal education and practice. For instance, in Western Uttar Pradesh, 107, 40, and 67 law institutions are connected with three state universities of Meerut, Agra, and Kanpur respectively. Over 25,000 seats are available in the LLB degree program at these 214 law colleges, which seems to make them more of fee collection offices rather than academic institutions. The stratification of law schools into different legal, regulatory, institutional, and governance frameworks has made it extremely difficult for most law schools to set high standards of instruction and create a conducive academic environment.

(c) According to the statistics shared by Dr. E. Vijay Kumar, there are more than 500,000 lawyers in the nation; while 40,000 law graduates receive degrees each year, and only 5% of those graduates become effective attorneys. These numbers amply reflect the quality of legal education in India.

(d) As per independent research, "The Bar Council of India (BCI) affiliated 74 new law colleges between 1 April 2020 and 31 March 2021. Approximately, 240 college affiliations for the year 2019 without giving due consideration to the needs of the profession or the availability of suitable opportunities for young law graduates (around 20 new colleges affiliated per month). Worse, these numbers would have been much more had the BCI not imposed a three-year moratorium on opening new law colleges, in its resolve to improve the standards of existing law colleges. Sadly, many of the current institutions constitute a "profit-making industry" where a part-time lecturer imparts instructions to classrooms packed with disinterested students, where college attendance is only a perfunctory activity, not for the love of the subject.

(e) According to BCI statistics, there are around 1,500 law colleges across the country, with private colleges making up for 75%, approx. There are 7 million registered lawyers in the country, and 80,000 to 100,000 new advocates are enrolled annually. And approximately, one million two hundred thousand lawyers of the two million lawyers in the country are fake, as reported by Sarda (2017).

(f) While hearing a challenge to Section 9 of the Advocates Act in September last year, the Madras High Court reiterated the long-standing concern over the proliferation of sub-standard law colleges. Chief Justice Sanjib Banerjee had previously called them "cowshed law colleges" urging for a quick redressal of the menace.

(g) In January 2018, Justices Arun Mishra and Mohan Shantangoudar of the Supreme Court aptly observed, "You cannot open (private law) colleges like this. There should be some restrictions. One person cannot have ten children."

(h) The Madras High Court held in 2017 that 85% of law colleges must be closed to maintain the sanctity of the legal profession.

(i) A pathbreaking survey undertaken by the Research Foundation for Governance in India (RFGI) observes that "there is a complete lack of coordination between the norms of BCI, UGC, and the Government as far as legal education is concerned. The position of law colleges is that of a 'sandwich' between the rules of the BCI, the UGC, and the Government, who are unable to impart quality legal education.

(j) Despite the BCI's obligation to promote legal education and lay down 'standards', it has failed to carry out the 'consultation process' with the universities. High-time BCI acknowledged that those who work full-time in legal education are best suited to define norms. Former Prime Minister Dr. Manmohan Singh succinctly summed up the sorry state of affairs when he stated, "Indian legal education is characterised by a few islands of excellence amidst a sea of institutionalised mediocrity."

5.2   Enormity and Mediocrity of the Applicant Pool

The quality of a school's student body has a strong influence on the quality of the education imparted. Until about 1995, students often turn to law as a last resort after failing to secure admission to medical, engineering, or commerce programmes. By merely filling vacant seats, a Law College unknowingly plays a significant role in lowering the standard of legal education in India.

The following observations and instances throw more light on this problem:

(a) The Supreme Court recently ruled that "anti-social elements" were graduating with a degree in law without attending a single class. The bench emphasised that although BCI is authorised under the law to prescribe criteria for admission to law schools and enrolment of lawyers, the current situation requires an intervention by the top court.

(b) For several reasons, it can be said that legal education and profession are overcrowded. In 2020, Justice N. Kirubakaran of the Madras High Court cited instances of fake attendance records and fraudulent issuance of bona fide certificates to students to get students enrolled as lawyers in the Bar Council of Tamil Nadu and Puducherry.

(c) Attendance is another crucial factor, which plays a key role in the degradation of legal education in India and its applicant pool. As per rule 4 of the Bar Council of India (Part IV), "The student shall be requested to put minimum attendance of 66% of a lecture on each of the subject as also at the moot courts practical training course. The provision of compulsory attendance remains on paper and is hardly enforced.

(d) A large number of students join the Law (LL.B) course devoid of a serious objective to pursue a career in law. A case in point is the three-year law course, where students of colleges located in rural or far-off places also pursue a job, business, or other courses in parallel. We also have a serious situation where one college maintains the standard and another does not, which creates a glaring disparity among the law colleges of the country.

(e) Many law colleges in India are not serious and professional about imparting education to students pursuing a three-year law degree. This is especially the case with many privately held academic institutions providing legal education mainly given the focus on the five-year law degree students who pay higher fees compared to three-year law degree students. This tendency is grossly unfair to three-year law degree students.

(f) Worse, the three-year legal degrees are neither offered nor accepted at the different publicly financed National Law Schools of India, such as the National Law School of India University (NLSIU) in Bengaluru and the NALSAR University in Hyderabad. Consequently, three-year law degrees have become a playground for privately held institutions that offer legal education as a business venture. Many of these institutions charge higher fees for all degrees compared to the NLSIU or the NALSA without adding any value in terms of education imparted.

(g) Law schools that offer the three-year course invariably draw in students of a very low calibre, which negatively impacts the practical applications of the law degree. This also leads to employability issues which, in turn, leads to significant unemployment. Although one can start a private practice with a professional degree, doing so is very difficult for recent law graduates, especially if their education is of subpar quality.

5.3 Mockery of Entrance Examination

Admissions to law Schools in India have been subject to students clearing the following entrance examination. Unfortunately, there are too many such tests and they are becoming difficult every day. Whilst one cannot find fault with the admission test, these tests actually do not test the 'aptitude' of the students on his/her acumen to become a lawyer. For example, lawyering is all about, (a) the capability to find solutions with an open mind, (b) having the patience to listen carefully (without any bias), (c) being ready and willing to 'learn' and 'apply' all throughout the practice, and (d) ability to be precise in articulation whether verbal or in writing. It is unfortunate that NO Law School Admission test even attempts to find out these traits in the students who wish to pursue law as their career. Scoring good marks or securing admission to any good law school is no guarantee that he/she will be a successful lawyer in his/her career.

Candidates who wish to take up Law as a career need to qualify for any of the entrance examinations listed below:

(a) CET- Common Entrance Test is conducted by Guru Govind Singh Indraprastha University, Dwarka, New Delhi for various courses it offers including Five Year Law Courses of BBA LLB and BA LLB.

(b) CLAT- Common Law Admission Test, commonly known as CLAT is the national level law entrance exam.

(c) LSAT- Law School Admission Test, commonly known as LSAT is a standardized test of reading and verbal reasoning skills designed by the USA–based Law School Admission Council (LSAC) for use by law schools in India. http://www.pearsonvueindia.com/lsatindia/

(d) DU LLB/LLM - Faculty of Law, Delhi University conducts a separate law entrance exam for admissions to various law courses namely LLB and LLM courses. is- Symbiosis Entrance Test commonly known as SET is a commonly written test conducted for taking admission to undergraduate law programs offered by various institutes under Symbiosis International University.

(e) ULSAT- UPES Law Studies Aptitude Test commonly known as ULSAT is conducted by the University of Petroleum and Energy Studies (UPES). The competitive entrance test is conducted to grant admission to Bachelor of Laws (B.A. LLB) and LLB in Corporate Laws, Cyber Laws, and Intellectual Property Rights.

The aptitude of the examinee is not tested in the current entrance examination system in a way that accurately reflects his or her capacity to be a competent lawyer. While CLAT focuses on topics like Mathematics, General Knowledge, Legal Aptitude, and others, the LSAT analyses a candidate's reasoning and critical thinking ability, which is good but needs a more scientific approach and detailed analysis. The affinity for law needs to be identified if not the ability but the entrance exam largely ignores this vital area.

The English language is given an excessive amount of attention in a nation where the majority of pupils are not exposed to it throughout their formative years of education.

Several CLAT portions demand that applicants have an in-depth understanding of subjects including criminal law, tort law, contract law, and Indian constitutional law. The expectation of prior knowledge in these areas defeats the purpose when the goal is to provide significant education in the said areas throughout undergraduate study.

CLAT exams are marked by serious discrepancies in terms of allocation of seats, release of merit lists, maladministration, and policy inconsistencies. Unless this is radically changed, we will never get the right students in the legal profession and the majority of students will never get their right deserving career.

5.4   Substandard Teaching Facilities and Techniques

The traditional Socratic/lecture method continues to be a prevalent mode of instruction at most institutions with large numbers of students, limited faculty experience and expertise, and inadequate infrastructure facilities. There is a strong need for imparting holistic knowledge enriched by practical experience and individual perspectives. The situation on the ground leaves a lot to be desired.

Most law schools adopt the conventional approach of one-way lecturing to large groups of students, thereby promoting rote learning and largely closing the doors to experiential learning. Students tend to become passive listeners and learning outcomes are suboptimal. Few teachers have any experience in efficient lecture delivery.

It is high time we paid heed to Prof. Baxi's proposals of 1974 to establish a Legal Pedagogy Institute to offer programmes for faculty development and teacher training. For judges, attorneys, and academics, knowing the law must be a continuous endeavour in order to adapt to the changes taking place all around us.

The Ormrod Committee (1971) placed a strong emphasis on the need to impart training in professional skills and techniques as the legal profession relied heavily on the conventional apprenticeship method. It recommended "the merging of academic and professional teaching materials into a coherent whole" and proposed three levels of legal education: (i) the academic stage; (ii) the professional stage, which includes both institutional training and in-training; and (iii) ongoing education or training.

A fine blend between the active method i.e. the case method, also known as the Langdell method, and the passive method i.e. the lecture method, is the need of the hour. The first three years can be devoted to the traditional teaching of both substantive and processual laws by employing both the active (case law) and passive (lecture) methods. Those students who do not desire to practise law or who do not aspire to a judicial career may terminate their studies with an ordinary law degree. Those who desire to enter the profession as law practitioners or aspire for judicial service may be bifurcated into two distinct streams. The training in these two streams may be in certain specialised subjects for one year with a shift in emphasis depending on the stream chosen. Till the completion of the fourth year, a student may be allowed to change his stream. The last year would be devoted to giving intensive and extensive training in the skills and techniques of the chosen discipline, i.e. a professional career or a judicial career.

5.5 Good and Experienced Teachers – Perennially in short supply

In general, law schools have trouble motivating talented lawyers to work as professors in their programmes (even part-time). The pre-requisite of NET-qualified applicants as lecturers has consistently come in the way of hiring excellent professionals as teachers. This is a serious lacuna in legal education. Further, some law schools also force professors to teach subjects in which they lack knowledge which makes a mockery of the teaching standards.

Most of the law teachers join the law schools after completing their LL.B., LL.M. or Ph.D. and are rarely (literally none) exposed to the practical aspect of law and the courts. Such teachers impart theoretical knowledge, divorced from the practical aspects and the result is that a fresh lawyer appears quite lost in the courtroom battles or any transactional or advisory work.

The NALSAR report pointed out that most NLUs have on average engaged 30 - 40% of their full-time teachers on an 'ad-hoc' or 'visiting' basis. Only three NLUs engaged more than 80% of their faculty members in permanent positions. At most NLUs, the non-teaching staff members largely occupy temporary positions. Even private law universities (PLUs) prefer contractual appointments to enable a culture of 'hire and fire' talent as and when deemed necessary." This policy is merely to accommodate or avoid the financial burden of permanent professors on the institutions which is equally a serious issue when it comes to their own careers as academicians.

The National Knowledge Commission has recommended salary differentials within and between universities and law schools to help retain quality talent and promote a culture of excellence. It has also recommended incentives like increasing existing promotional schemes and avenues to promote faculty members, providing fully paid sabbaticals and adequate House Rent Allowance (HRA); instituting awards to honour reputed teachers and researchers at national and international levels, and allowing faculty to take up consultancy assignments and legal practice in courts. But will the recommendations ever see the light of day is anybody's guess.

Full-time law teachers fail to impart practical training and clinical experiences to students due to a lack of experience at the bar or in any law firm. Strangely enough, a practising advocate may teach law as a part-time lecturer, but a full-time faculty cannot practice law, though he/she may seek permission to appear in a particular case.

A national institute of legal education should be formed with the goal of offering intensive teacher-training programmes. Law schools with sufficient resources should hire practising attorneys/in-house counsel as part-time instructors. The University Grants Commission (UGC) should also explore the possibility of offering attorneys six to twelve-month professional leave to pursue their teaching passion.

Most importantly, clinical law teachers should be given due credit and recognition for their efforts in deciding their selections and promotions. It is an undeniable fact that law schools can attract many good students towards legal education only when the faculty members have the right blend of academic knowledge, practical experience, and work proficiency.

5.6 Law School Syllabus – The Achilles Heel

There hasn't been much innovation in the legal education landscape, save for a stretch in the length of the courses and the introduction of a few core disciplines. Most law schools stick to an outdated and traditional pedagogy at the cost of not keeping pace with evolving and emerging industry trends. Law colleges do not play an active role in law-making to deal with issues that could arise in the future. A classic example is that of the laws governing information technology and the business/transactions that are carried out over the internet. Whilst India boasts about being the country with the largest penetration of the internet, we failed to frame stronger and comprehensive laws dealing with data privacy or cybercrimes.

In 1996, the United Nations Commission on International Trade Law (UNCITRAL) adopted the model law on electronic commerce (e-commerce) to bring uniformity in the law in different countries. Further, the General Assembly of the United Nations recommended that all countries must consider this model law before making changes to their own laws. India became the 12th country to enable cyber law after it passed the Information Technology Act, 2000.

Project submission is marred by the practice of giving students good marks despite the rampant copy-pasted, plagiarized submissions. The lame justification put forth is that it helps students get jobs and find LLM seats in foreign universities but beyond big grants and tall claims, there is no meaningful continuing education imparted.

BCI has listed 18 compulsory papers and a hoard of optional papers, but the formulation of the syllabus is left to the universities. This leads to a clumsy situation of varied syllabi across the country for a law that is uniform across the country.

There is an acute need for a paradigm shift - from a traditional curriculum that is litigation-focused to one that places a higher emphasis on problem-solving, negotiation, and transactional practice. The curriculum needs to put a theoretical as well as practical emphasis on

Curriculum development is ideally a continual process, which merits the proactive collaboration of regulatory agencies, law schools, and legal educators to sharpen its relevance and significance. BCI's prior approach of forcing a curriculum on law schools defeated the purpose. Thankfully, it has now recognised the need to promote faculty autonomy in the design and implementation of the updated curriculum, which is scheduled to be implemented soon.

the inculcation of the identity, values and dispositions consonant with the fundamental purposes of legal education.

With regard to the medium of instruction, the Bar Council holds that English must be used at all law schools. The decision on the language of instruction should be left up to universities and law schools as our constitution guarantees linguistic justice to all. More importantly, the majority of people who seek justice in the first instance go to subordinate courts, where proceedings are invariably conducted in the regional language.

Even the top most law schools of India are ranked in the 151-200 band as per the QS World University Subject Rankings 2020 which explains the sorry state of affairs.

5.7 Conventional Examination System – Need to test for jurisprudential skills

Like the entrance test exam, even each semester examinations during the five-year or three-year law course need to undergo serious changes.

Laws schools use the conventional testing format. In college, the evaluation or capability criteria are based on memorising a small portion of the prescribed syllabus plus a few questions from the previous year's tests. Instead of reflecting their analytical and practical skills, students' report cards are a reflection of their capacity to memorise a small number of sections, articles, facts, case laws, etc.

While having a good memory is undoubtedly a great benefit for lawyers, proficiency cannot be judged solely on the basis of recollection skills. The exam must also gauge a law student's proficiency in language comprehension, critical thinking, research orientation, factual understanding, application of mind and solution-oriented approach besides oral and written communication, which has to be precise and to the point.

Traditional institutions use the relatively simple route by using example question banks and solutions that are printed and offered for sale at stationery stores. Students can be confident that no questions from sources other than the publication will be posed during the exam because some publications release sample answers to these questions.

The majority of graduates from well-known universities who worked as attorneys before passing the bar did not perform well academically during their time in law school. Instead, they grasped more knowledge working as advocates' interns and learning professional skills that the legal education system ignored, even as a means of evaluation. There are umpteen examples of highly successful lawyers and solicitors in India and even abroad who were academically very poor but did extremely well in their professional careers in achieving name and fame. Even several judges across India who were not the brightest law students but have delivered outstanding decisions and developed jurisprudence on various subjects.

Questions in subjects like Constitutional law should ideally sharpen theoretical and jurisprudential skills. Substantive laws, such as the Indian Penal Code, should have research-oriented questions that force the student to conduct an interdisciplinary study in criminology, victimology, justice studies, etc. A paper in Intellectual Property Rights (IPR) that encourages students to apply for or work toward obtaining patent, copyright, geographic indication, or certification of traditional knowledge for products they believe should be treated at par with academic research work under the supervision of the professors. The examinee should be required to create plaints and SLPs for procedural legislation including the civil and criminal procedure statutes.

Most first-year law students are often clueless when they first mark their presence in a District Court. Many students drop out of law schools in between and even after graduation for want of practical exposure. The examinations need to be more practice-based and also make it very clear to them the expectations of the profession once they graduate.

5.8 Paradigm Shift – Foreign Universities and Legal Professionals in India

A key question has recently surfaced in legal education: Why should a student attend Indian law schools when foreign degrees may be obtained at the same cost? Clearly, the rampant globalisation of society and the development of internet technologies provide a greater threat to national sovereignty than before.

It must be recognized that law has moved from internationalization to transnationalization to globalization. Legal practice should, therefore, move forward from an exclusive focus on litigation, arbitration, and compliance to problem-solving and structuring collaborations and joint ventures and management of international legal affairs. To operate effectively in a globalized legal market, individual lawyers need to be adept at multiple jurisdictions, often simultaneously.

Law schools should hence, impart training in identifying and appropriately responding to issues of cultural sensitivities. More collaboration and discussions among faculty and students across countries will stimulate debate and discussion on crucial aspects of law and legal education.

Despite the fact that all foreign law schools can establish branches in India, only the degrees in law from some universities abroad enjoy recognition by the Bar Council of India. Other universities need to go through complex negotiations. The diversity of educational initiatives can increase healthy competition and improve the quality of education, but can it touch the lives of ordinary Indians and improve their access to legal services is a debatable issue.

5.9 Collaboration – The missing key link

To help diversify areas of research and cultivate student capacity to contribute to other fields, it is imperative to promote collaboration between law schools and various institutions and organisations, including corporations, non-governmental organisations, municipalities, and the Parliament. External partnerships are the most effective way to achieve clinical legal education, such as on legal assistance, access to justice, pro bono services, professional obligations and ethics, and moot court contests.

In countries like the United States, Australia, China and Brazil, legal education incorporates international collaboration as the norm. In sharp contrast, India has still not recognised the critical importance of transnational education.

Collaborating with an urban planner, visiting the slum cluster facing eviction, sitting down with its inhabitants there to discuss the case filed for them in the High Court, planning strategies, and appraising them of the developments after each hearing can be a huge learning experience for students.

5.10   The glaring disparity among law institutions

Key holistic and inclusive reforms are the need of the hour across central and state university law departments, affiliated law colleges, and the deemed and private universities.

The gap between "elite" educational institutions and commonplace institutions has grown significantly due to the great divide in cultures and educational methods. The corporatization of legal education has seen many business houses setting up private law universities with ample seat availability and customized admissions procedures. Some of these PLUs charge tuition fees far higher than NLU fees. Universities have been giving affiliations generously, and state governments are issuing No Objection Certificates. In most rural locations, universities are powerless to halt the use of dishonest exam practices and state governments choose to look the other way.

None of the Indian law schools find a place in the top 300 law schools of the world as per the QS World University Subject Rankings 2019. NIUs combined impart legal education to only about 2,500 students in a year, which is not even 2% of the total LLB students admitted to Indian law colleges in a year.

5.11   Clinical Legal Aid Cell – Startling Facts

The United States and Australia follow a rigorous, clinical legal education, which involves first-hand practical knowledge to sharpen the legal acumen of students. Law students are placed in legal clinics and allowed to play the role of an actual lawyer for real clients, representing them in the Courts of Law. Many universities in Australia like the University of New South Wales (UNSW), the University of South Australia and the University of Newcastle have their own legal clinics on campus for their students to indulge in clinical training.

A joint study conducted in 2011 by the V M Salgaocar Law College, the Forum of South Asian Clinical Law Teachers, the Government of India and the United Nations Development in seven States chose seven Indian law colleges across different states for 'best practices' in devising outreach programmes to bring legal services to the doorstep of the rural poor by locating some of the legal aid clinics in rural regions. However, despite the fact that nearly 82% of the 38 law schools had designated faculty to conduct legal aid activity in the clinics, only a minuscule part of them provided the facility of academic credit to the faculty in terms of workload/ lecture hours and for the students in terms of grades or marks. This, in turn, considerably reduced the enthusiasm for legal aid activity. The need for a fool-proof clinical legal education in India cannot hence be over-emphasised.

5.12   Burden of Student Loans and the Shift in Favour of Corporate Jobs

In one of his speeches, the highly eminent justice Dhananjaya Y. Chandrachud rightly observed, "The prospect of high-paying corporate jobs at the end of the law course has changed who applies to law schools, the choice of law schools, the educational experience at law schools, and how much students are willing to pay for legal education. The financial return from working in a law firm comes much sooner than it does in litigation, making the investment in legal education a less risky investment for the young. Hence, deviating from the originally stated objective of improving the bar and the bench, the NLU became a means of providing employees to law firms, aspiring lawyers aimed to gain entrance into NLU, in order to secure a job in a reputed, high-paying law firm." This trend of NLU churning possible recruits for law firms is evident from the law school rankings, which are in large part determined by recruitment in the corporate sector.

The fees for enrolling for NLU are significantly high, and students often take jobs with law firms and corporations in order to repay loans.

A 2018 report by NALSAR observed, "The institutions that were meant to be the torchbearers of systemic reform are producing graduates which are diverted towards lucrative opportunities in the private sector while the older institutions continue to be run with laxity. This has exacerbated the career ambivalence that has always existed in India's legal profession. At the top of the legal education pyramid, we have a small group of highly selective institutions that have become feeders for the leading commercial law firms and business entities while a vast majority of law departments and colleges continue to add to the pool of 'briefless barristers' and graduates who will never use their law degree to earn a living."

In 2014, Jonathan Gingerich and Nick Robinson noted in their study titled 'Responding to the Market: The Impact of the Rise of Corporate Law Firms on Elite Legal Education in India' that: "The impact of the corporate sector on elite legal education in India has become increasingly apparent as more and more graduates enter law firms and the administration and faculty of law schools navigate how they wish to situate themselves and their students in relation to this lucrative section of the legal market." Gingerich and Robinson noted that the choice that students in the NLUs make about which courses they will opt for is dictated largely by the prospect of securing a corporate desk job. They gravitate toward electives that they think are likely to prove attractive to recruiters from law firms and in turn "have pushed their law schools to offer more such electives." The head of an elite law school was candid that "when students have an opportunity to choose electives, eighty per cent will take Mergers and Acquisitions over International Humanitarian Law because students and their parents think that completing course work on corporate subjects will make it easier to secure placement into a corporate desk job."

For underprivileged students, especially those attending less prestigious schools or who perform poorly in their studies, large loans have substantial consequences. Although some law schools are able to place almost all of their students in jobs that generate income adequate to pay off debts, many are unable to, and it may be challenging to place the students who need the biggest loans in high-paying, major corporations in big cities. Due to their low-paying positions in litigation, the majority of students end up in a loop of financial burden and decide to work for corporations instead.

5.13 Demons of Elitism

The fee schedules at the NLU are significantly higher than those at the colleges and law schools affiliated with the top public universities. This creates the impression that the NLUs are solely accessible to the wealthiest sections of society even though they are public institutions. An NLU survey conducted in 2015–16 found glaring underrepresentation among pupils from rural areas, those attending schools where Indian language instruction is the norm, and those who identify as religious minorities.

Over 80% of the students enrolling at NLUs come from wealthy, urban, and English-speaking homes as per the findings of the 2018-19 report. In NLUs, the typical course fee (including boarding costs and tuition) ranges between Rs. 15 and 18 lakhs while in PLUs, it could be as high as Rs. 28 lakhs annually. More than 85% of the students in the sample had registered in pricey coaching programmes or online courses to get ready for the CLAT. Only 9% of the students chose to take bank loans, while over 88% of them were funded by their parents.

5.14   Drafting – A largely ignored skill

Drafting pleadings or contracts is one of the most essential skill sets for both lawyers and law students. However, law colleges don't teach drafting skills like litigation-related drafting or high-end agreements related to mergers and acquisitions, foreign collaborations, joint ventures, partnerships or general corporate contract drafting. As mentioned earlier, there is an acute need for a paradigm shift – from a traditional curriculum that is general litigation or compliance-focused toward one that places a higher emphasis on problem-solving, negotiation, and corporate transactional practice. To meet the rising demand for cross-border legal services brought on by globalisation, lawyers must not only command a knowledge of various national, international, and supranational legal systems, economies and cultures but also be skilled in structuring partnerships, technical and financial collaborations, problem-solving, negotiation, and transactional techniques. Many cross-border legal issues can be resolved without resorting to courtroom litigation if proper planning and agreements are made in advance. Hence, the pivotal importance of contract drafting skills.

5.15   Teaching Law as a Profession – Stumbling Roadblocks

Sadly, many factors including substantial financial costs, the plain vanilla nature of the job, and lack of motivation from disinterested and superficial law instructors deter some of the finest students from pursuing teaching careers in law. This needs to change.

The motive behind establishing more colleges is only to gain profit, hence they purposefully keep teacher remuneration to the bare minimum.

Consequently, unqualified and part-time teachers impart education to students which has a fatal impact on the motivation of the students.

Full-time professors typically make far less money than law firm partners in most metropolitan cities. The starting associate salary in the big firms in many cities is less than the median assistant professor's income. It is pertinent to note that when compared to the difference between the incomes of associates and partners, the difference between the median earnings of assistant and full professors is minuscule.

Yet another sad fact is that a law professor's responsibilities are the same at age 70 as they were at age 25. The only way a law professor can advance professionally, in contrast to a partner in private practice, is through legal scholarship or moonlighting. The constricted opportunities for growth and advancement are the reason for a perennial lack of good professors in universities.

Chapter 6

My Journey as Corporate Lawyer

"Don't believe what your eyes are telling you. All they show is limitation. Look with your understanding, find out what you already know, and you'll see the way to fly."

- Richard Bach, author of Jonathan Livingston Seagull

When I returned from my business trip to London at the end of February 2020, little did I know that the world was about to face a catastrophe of unprecedented size and scale, a calamity that was to change our lives and livelihoods forever, in ways we would not have imagined even in our wildest nightmares. Come March 2020, COVID-19 formally announced its arrival. It was clear by then that this toxic virus was a ruthless predator intent on playing havoc, although it was acknowledged as a pandemic much later.

This abrupt home confinement was a unique experience for countless professionals like me – a mandatory sabbatical of introspection and intrigue – that was thrust on us without prior intimation by forces beyond our control. During this period of lull, when I was searching for 'everything' in the name of 'something', I came across a gem in a book from: 'Jonathan Livingston Seagull' written by pilot-turned-barnstormer-turned-celebrated author, Richard Bach. I have lost count of how many times I read this four-part book ever since.

It was perhaps the outwardly simple but magnificently profound message that deeply resonated with me. Bach, who is spiritually fixated on flying and aviation as his chosen transcendental themes, tells a poignantly inspirational story of a starry-eyed seagull named Jonathan Livingston Seagull who dares to dream of those very things his folks have dismissed as being futile and unwarranted. While his mates chase the boats lured by the prospect of savouring scattered fish scraps and littered breadcrumbs, Jonathan takes to the skies to practice the dedication and discipline of flying. His love for the skies comes with a heavy penalty – he is expelled from his tribe and made an outcast, but that doesn't deter him from soaring higher in the guiding light of two seasoned gulls. Jonathan returns to his people to share the art and science of flying and spread love against all odds, as instructed by his Guru. Braving the initial resentment and flippancy of the natives, he imparts his experiential wisdom to a few aspiring gulls, helps them see the virtues beneath the veil, and leaves for new shores after the new flocks have become adept at flying. Towards the end of the parable, Jonathan is predictably converted into a God by his community, and most gulls spend most time in blind worship and ostensible devotion. Soon after, a few birds shun the confines of conformity and take to flying with the vigour it demands. But there's a gull called Anthony who is consumed by the apparent futility of life and decides to end his life. However, he is motivated to think otherwise in the nick of time by an enigmatic, angelic gull who appears from nowhere, and when asked for his name, only says, "You can call me Jon!" This suggestive end is so powerful in its metaphorical imagery and unpretentious sermon that sincere readers can't help but seek to discover the Jonathan Livingston Seagull in them and appreciate the relevance in their respective lives.

Every time I read the book, I go back in time to recount the cherished milestones of my personal voyage of over 30 years – my school and college time, graduation span, law college days, internship interview, initial days of practice, golden time spent with my seniors, and career highs and lows as a corporate M&A lawyer! I have knowingly and unknowingly identified with Jonathan Livingston Seagull, in contemplative hindsight, as I try to connect the dots of the proverbial line that has brought me to where I find myself today. Like Jonathan, I have suffered the pangs of discontentment with the humdrum of life, the misery of isolation and helplessness led by the craving to chart an education and career of choice, the unconditional love and support from my mentors at every decisive juncture, the need to be grounded at all times, and the urge to give back to the community by sharing what I have learnt over the years, whether from my seniors or from sheer experience.

Today, when I look back, I find great satisfaction in having delivered the lecture series on, (a) M&A and Joint Ventures, and (b) Lawyers in Making over a span of more than two decades on diverse platforms – whether various law schools, or various fraternity meets.

However, I have experienced a deeper sense of fulfilment in the articulation of my home-grown experiences and insights, in the form of a new corporate theory titled 'The GPS Paradigm for Successful Mergers, acquisitions and joint ventures' (published in 2021), to help existing and future business leaders and decision-makers deal with the diktats of disruptive technology and perpetual unpredictability in the course of designing and implementing their M&A and JVs.

However, during my interactions with young, aspiring lawyers, I realized that there's an entirely different set of challenges they face – challenges not covered in the standard law school curriculum. From the daunting task of gaining admission to a prestigious law school to the rigorous grind of moot courts, internships, and the ultimate quest for a fulfilling career in the legal world, the journey of a law student is fraught with questions and uncertainties.

This realization led me to address these budding legal minds in my lectures titled "Lawyers in Making." Here, I endeavoured to unravel the intricacies of law education, offering guidance on how to maximize the law school experience and chart a successful path post-graduation. Recognizing the need for a more comprehensive guide, I embarked on writing the "Companion Handbook for Law Students" soon after publishing my first book. This handbook is designed to be a pragmatic, insightful guide, addressing the unspoken yet crucial aspects of legal education in India.

My hope is that this book serves not only as a guide for current law students but also as a valuable resource for those who have recently graduated and are on the cusp of starting their legal careers, whether as lawyers, general counsels, or in-house counsels. It is crafted for the mavericks, the changemakers of tomorrow, who aspire to be more than just participants in the legal realm – they aim to be the very embodiment of change itself.

"In a gentle way, you can shake the world." – Mahatma Gandhi

Family upbringing and formative education play a vital role in shaping one's personal and professional development. In my case, the playground of life together with the classroom of my alma mater have provided me with a rich ammunition of actionable insights, which have proved handy in sustaining and celebrating many an umpteen trial and triumph of my corporate law career. I almost feel duty-bound to share a few pages of my life book before I come to charting the trajectory of my law career in the specific context of M&As, Joint Ventures and Collaborations. I am more than sure that budding professionals across different spheres will find my experiences handy in charting their own careers, through a conscious resolve to learn from the bagful of lessons that I have learnt over the years: the blunders that could have been nipped in the bud, the things that I did right, as also the umpteen trials and triumphs of my career as a corporate lawyer.

I am a first-generation lawyer. Before me, no one from my family had anything to do with law. So, when my astrologer uncle predicted that I would become a lawyer, all were taken by surprise. But my uncle's prophecy came bundled with his basic familiarity with the legal profession. Well aware of the distinction between Chamber practice and Counsel practice, he insisted that I should do Chamber practice, not conduct suits and court actions. So, one can say I was kind of destined to become a lawyer! Given a choice, I would have loved to become an Architect, although I have thoroughly relished my career as a corporate lawyer.

6.1   Highs and Lows of Early Life

On the 21st day of February 1963, exactly three months after the end of the Sino-Indian war, I was born to a middle-class family in a locality inhabited by the Kutchi people (an enterprising business community widely spread across the globe) in the Mumbai suburb of Mulund. I learnt to speak and write fluent Gujarati from my neighbours, a lingo that has kept me in good stead throughout my profession. My father worked as a senior typewriter mechanic at the Godrej & Boyce Manufacturing Co. Ltd. while my mother was a devoted housewife. We lived a very simple but happy life. My doting mother always wanted her children – two elder brothers and I – to study hard and prosper in life. My father was blessed with a good singing voice, its silken quality resembling that of the famous playback artiste, Talat Mehmood. Every year during Diwali, I spent a good time at his office typing something or the other on his typewriter. I never ceased to be amazed by the sight of hundreds of typewriters at the Godrej manufacturing plant.

My elder brother studied at the Sampson English High School. I have fond memories of the school, as captured by my roving eyes as a small child. My mom always took me along while carrying tiffin for my brother during recess. I was always in awe of my well-groomed brother in the school uniform. He introduced me to the English alphabets and numbers, much before I was enrolled in the same school, which is linked to a story in itself.

I would have been four at that time. I was seated at the table in the office of the principal, Mrs. S. S. Sampson who had called my mom for a meeting. All of a sudden, I began uttering the English alphabets and numbers from 1 to 100 as if I were appearing for an admission test. The principal, all ears to my abrupt recitation, instantly asked my mom to enrol me in the same school. My mother was very happy to hear what she heard but quietly submitted, "We may not be able to afford the school fees." The kind-hearted principal immediately offered a 50% discount for my fees right till standard V. This was how my schooling began, with quite a flourish, and a bumper discount!

Mrs. Sampson was an Israeli lady known for her upright behaviour and hard discipline. Among other things, she taught us the significance of time, dress code, respect, and cleanliness. Thanks to her, these core values have stayed with me to date. I am deeply pained if, for whatever reason, I am unable to make it to a meeting at the scheduled time, or if I am not immaculately dressed up in line with the given occasion.

From the age of 14 till the time I completed my law graduation, I became financially independent in my own right, managing my fees and personal expenses by giving tuition to small kids. The irony of this whole affair was striking – at the age of 15, in the last year of school, I earned almost Rs. 750 per month. In stark contrast, after seven years, when I was a law graduate at the age of 24,

It's high time Indian law firms adopted a basic minimum pay besides improving the apprenticeship working conditions through a structured and practical syllabus. In fact, given the Covid-imposed lockdown, online internship programs must be allowed to run parallel to conventional education, not just for law students but for probationers across engineering, architectural, accounting and all other professions which put a premium on experiential learning.

I was fetching a meagre Rs. 500 per month as an internship stipend. This is an extremely unfortunate reality of the legal profession in India. The scene is yet dismal in the legacy law firms though most new firms now pay a decent amount for internships.

6.2 Science to Economics: a wanton winding route

I must share a monumental blunder of mine that happened at a crucial stage of my life. In a career, one is expected to take a right turn invariably and occasionally even turn left, but there are times when one should have the courage to take a U-turn if one approaches a dead end. The right path, no matter how long it takes to embark on it, will more than makeup for the time lost, that is my assurance to all aspirants, regardless of the career stream.

Enthused by the financial rewards of conducting tuition throughout my student years, as also urged by my elder brother, I opted for the science stream post-matriculation. The whole and sole idea behind this choice was that science education would phenomenally bolster my tuition earnings. Honestly, I was keen on taking up commerce because it was the most logical route leading to law graduation. (In fact, I ended up securing admissions in both science and commerce streams in Vani Vidyalaya & Jr. College, Mulund, adjacent to my Sampson School).

My tryst with science met the expected fate. I was not good at Math, but somehow cleared XI and XII exams to join the Ramniranjan Jhunjhunwala College, Ghatkopar, for my Bachelor of Science graduation. I knew very well my career plans were going haywire but now, I then felt, there was no looking back and simply let the conundrum grow to alarming proportions. Initially, I took Physics and Biology as my major subjects but later changed them to Physics and Math to escape the rigours of Biology practicals. After suffering an agonizing six months, I reached the boiling point beyond which I could take no more. One fine day, I simply put the terminal full stop to my science graduation in my mind even though I was attending college. I was downright depressed but had no idea whom to approach for advice as there was no one who could comprehend my disillusionment, let alone show me the way out of my self-imposed confinement.

Just about that time, I saw some of my neighbours pursuing graduation in Arts from the renowned Ramnarain Ruia College of Arts, Matunga. Almost led by instinct, I decided to follow suit and enrolled for a graduation in Arts (Economics and Politics). During the admission process, a Sr. Student of Ruia called Dilip Patil was urging all of us to opt for Rural Development (RD) as an optional subject. He explained how easy it is to clear the subject since the written paper carries 60 marks while 40 marks are allocated for fieldwork. I happily followed his advice and ticked RD as the optional subject.

The decision proved a landmark for me as I was very happy to get invaluable insights into Rural India. In fact, at the age of 60, I completed my two years of Masters in RD. Here again, the same old Dilip Patil (now the HOD, Lifelong Learning and Extension at Mumbai University) offered me unconditional help. I now plan to complete my PhD in Rural Development under his guidance.

Coming back to my career, I swiftly completed my graduation in Arts with Economics and Politics as my major subjects. All waywardness was now behind me, and I **took** up my law studies with great enthusiasm and renewed vigour.

6.3 Hardship and Articleship hand in hand

I studied law at the well-known Government Law College, Churchgate, Mumbai. Established in 1855, it holds the distinction of being the oldest Law College in Asia. Most of my Ruia friends, probably in yet another play of destiny, wanted to become lawyers and solicitors. The peer pressure proved positive in my case as it was exactly about what I too wished to pursue.

I enjoyed my Law college time and particularly fancied 'Contract law' which was taught by my Principal, Mrs. Advani. In a cruel blow of fate, I failed in that very subject in the first year of LLB. Thankfully, I was declared passed on revaluation as the examiner had not assessed an entire supplement of my paper. However, I lost one semester (six months) due to the revaluation, needlessly lagging behind my friends. That was the first massive setback in my legal education. I re-joined college, determined to begin my career as a lawyer as soon as possible, but deep within, I was totally dejected.

Hence, the day I cleared my second year LLB in October 1988, I rushed to meet Prof. Dalmia in the lecturer's room with a request to allow me to join his chambers right away as I did not want to lose any more time. He conceded and thus began my career as a lawyer.

However, within two days, I cursed myself for the hasty decision as it would been more apt to join a bigger firm. Thankfully, my friends came to my rescue. They shared a few names of mid-sized law firms, one of which was M/s. V. A. Phadke & Co. I knew no one there, yet I called them up and spoke to the telephone operator, Mrs. Oak. Luckily, she happened to be a soft-spoken, compassionate lady. I asked her about joining as an articled clerk. I still don't know why but she immediately reassured me with unexpected warmth, "Yes, why not? Please come and meet Mr. V. A. Phadke, we have a lot of students working for us."

The next day at sharp 10, I was at their office. Mr. Phadke, an upright man probably in his 70s, looked at me and shot out a flurry of questions in a rather dismissive tone, "Who are you? Who gave you my name? Do you have any references? What do you know about my firm?" I told him I did not have any references as I was a first-generation lawyer. Then, I gave him very little background about myself.

He asked me to wait outside his cabin. Mrs. Oak offered me tea and I continued to wait all day. Around 5.00 p.m., Mr. Phadke came out of his cabin and was about to leave when his eyes fell on me. My heartbeats increased. He asked, "Are you still waiting? Did I not speak to you?" When he learnt that I had been waiting for that long, he seemed a bit apologetic and introduced me to his brother Mr. Bal Phadke before leaving the office.

After demanding a fresh round of introduction, his brother told me to come and meet him the next day. I was eager to know if that meant I was in. He was painfully non-committal and repeated, "Come tomorrow, we will talk again." Looking at my sullen face, Mrs. Oak tried to comfort me, "Don't worry, if he has asked you to come again, it means you are taken."

The next day, Mr. Bal Phadke asked me to meet Mr. V. A. Phadke. Just when my disappointment seemed to pave the way for frustration, I saw the elder Phadke greeting me with a smiling face for the first time. He said, "You may work under Mrs. Kanta Aiyer, who works in litigation." That was how my articleship began. In fact, I had no regular workspace in the office, so Mr. Phadke asked me to operate from the library. I was truly delighted as it gave me the freedom to read any book at any time. Mrs. Aiyer was a Gujarati married to a Tamil Chartered Accountant. I was proficient in Gujarati which helped establish a very cordial working relationship and I quickly learnt the ropes in her practice area. This experience gave me a ring-side view of civil and property litigation besides corporate work. I was very happy attending the celebrated Bombay High Court and the City Civil Court where I successfully handled a range of litigations including one matrimonial matter. That was indeed the golden period in the history of the Bombay High Court. Every day, I was at the office at sharp 9 a.m. By 11, I used to complete all routine work before rushing to the High Court to listen to arguments of senior counsel stalwarts like Ram Jethmalani, Fali Nariman, Soli Sorabjee, Arvind Sawant, Bhimrao Naik, and D. R. Dhanuka (the last three eventually became celebrated High Court Judges). I soaked in their wisdom wrapped in every word they used. I recollect having witnessed the trial of Shiv Sena Supremo Shri Bal Thackrey before Justice Bharucha where Ram Jethmalani and Adik Shirodkar argued for Shiv Sena in an election challenge on the issue of Hindutva. I also attended the Harshad Mehta hearings (Securities Scam of 1992) before the Special Court of Justice Variava.

6.4 Solicitor's exam: My four-year penance

I always had a burning desire to learn as many different subjects as possible, and that is the reason I always see myself as a student. Probably, that is also the reason that, years later, I did my Masters in Rural Development at the 'tender' age of 56! During graduation, I was happy to explore the depths of Economics, Politics and Marathi, ditto whilst learning 'Contract Law' at the Government Law College.

I passed law in 1989, but it was my keen desire to study law in depth, a yearning that was greatly satiated by my four attempts to clear the Solicitors Exam in May 1991. The reason for this protracted struggle was simple: I knew none of the committee members of the Incorporated Law Society which conducts the Solicitors Exam. Had I known any of them, I could have fetched some moral support as also the inspiration to put my best foot forward towards a methodical and comprehensive study.

I always knew that the Solicitors exam was extremely tough, with a passing percentage of 3 to 4%. Although the passing marks for each subject is 50%, one needs an average of 60% in the five subjects taken together to clear the exam. A preparation time of at least six months is an absolute must. In my first attempt, I failed to secure the aggregate by 11 marks! But I had no regrets as I thoroughly enjoyed studying for the second attempt as I got to see my subjects – chapter by chapter and section by section - in a new light. Unfortunately, I again failed in the second attempt too, clearing only two subjects: Companies Act and General Acts (open book exam). In my third attempt, I failed by a mere three marks in aggregate, but by this time, I was on the verge of giving it all up. I had neither the strength nor the inclination to study all over again.

This was easily the most depressing span of my career when only a handful of people encouraged me to stay put. It is indeed unfortunate that one has to struggle all the way to find a beacon of guiding light, someone who is expected to do simple things like merely encouraging you not to give up. This was also the time I entered into wedlock. My wife, Deepti, was a pillar of strength and support during these tough times; so was my father. He did not have the higher education to help me with my studies, but he definitely had maturity and empathy in good measure to help me tide over the crisis without losing my mind. Also, my inner voice told me I was almost there, so I should not be giving up. I shared my predicament with Raju Shah, a senior Solicitor (ex-Phadke). He told me once I cleared the exam, the number of attempts would not matter. It was my father's gospel, my wife's support, Raju Shah's encouragement, and my own tenacity that helped me touch the finish line. I distinctly remember I was in the Court Room of Justice Sujata Manohar when my Court Clerk barged in and conveyed the good news.

After completing the two years of articleship, I wanted to leave Mr. Phadke to join M/s. Shiralkar & Co., who had been Mr. Phadke's Junior. Mr. Phadke was sad to know of my decision, but he gave his approval without much ado. When I cleared my Solicitors Exam, he distributed sweets to one and all in his firm. To my knowledge, I was the last articled clerk under Mr. Phadke to pass the solicitor's exam. When I joined Mr. S. Y. Rege of Crawford Bayley (a close friend of Mr. Phadke), he was very happy as he had a very high regard for the firm.

I would like to emphasise one point for the benefit of young lawyers, chartered accountants, engineers, architects, or for that matter, any consultant: you may possibly have to change your path depending upon where your passion lies. Never lose heart. It may take some time to zero in on the right direction, but once you get on the right path, give it all you have! Always remember: your core knowledge, skills, and experience alone are your key working tools. Hence, you must strive to get a quality education, ideally a coveted degree from any good university or institution followed by a credible work experience under a veteran. Enjoy the learning process with an open mind even if it may eat into the initial years of your career. The blend of a good degree and an experienced mentor is an absolute must during your formative years. You reap what you sow! Your determination, tenacity, and commitment to your chosen sphere will together make all the difference.

6.5   Godrej and I: a career in absentia

Before I touch upon the Crawford Bayley chapter of my life, I must share the Godrej connection that has, in a very different, almost mystical sense, played a great role in my career development. Given my fascination with the typewriter, it was no surprise that I took to learning typing in a very formal manner, immediately after clearing my 11th standard. I passed the speed exam of 60 words per minute which was considered quite a feat in those days. When Godrej introduced 'feather touch' keys in its new 1980 typewriter model, the company was looking to recruit young people with better typing speeds. My father immediately asked me to apply for a job at Godrej. I passed the typing test and the personal interview. Just when I was all set to be recruited as a 'test typist,' I suddenly sensed my dream of becoming a lawyer fading away. So, deep within, I was not happy with the impending fate. I was almost in tears whilst giving my interview to one Mr. Patel.

But then, an anti-climax abruptly paved the way for my law career. At the time of signing the employment agreement, I was 17 years and 10 months, 2 months short of the mandatory age specification. Mr. Patel asked me to wait for two more months, by which time the vacancy was filled. So, I never joined Godrej.

Godrej came into my life yet again when I completed my BA graduation in economics and politics from Ramnarain Ruia College, Matunga. By the time I joined the Government Law College, Godrej launched an Electronic Typewriter. They were again looking for fresh graduates with a good knowledge of typing for their sales division. My father again asked me to apply while reassuring me that my law studies could continue in parallel. I was a bit disheartened but reluctantly applied for the post. Again, I cleared the initial rounds of interviews, but I guess they rejected me in the group discussion.

Once again, the rejection brought no dejection, and I focused on my law studies with renewed vigour.

Much later, after I had passed my Solicitors and joined Crawford Bayley, Godrej again came into the picture, but this time, I had knocked on its doors, in sheer dejection for a change. Despite being a law graduate armed with a Solicitors Degree, I was doing the monotonous work of old litigations, against my strong desire to work as a corporate lawyer. Consequently, I had made up my mind to join Godrej Soaps where a vacancy had been announced. But for the timely advice I got from the legal manager who interviewed me at Godrej Soaps, I changed my mind and stayed back at Crawford Bayley.

6.6   Crawford Bayley Chronicles: a rich reservoir of actionable insights

After conquering the exam front came the time to take the plunge into employment. By that time, I had identified Mr. R. A. Shah, Sr. Partner, Crawford Bayley (CB) as the topmost corporate lawyer in the country. I had made up my mind to work under him, but by the time I could apply, there was no vacancy at his office as someone else had already joined him.

I followed the advice of my friend Atul Rajyadhyaksha (now Sr. Counsel, High Court) and joined Senior Partner of CB S. Y. Rege in the litigation department, marking my entry into CB. Unfortunately, that debut year at CB proved extremely frustrating: while Mr. Shah's juniors did plum corporate work, I was doing musty litigation that had reached the final hearing stage. This was a cumbersome process as I had to first dust old files and then, struggle to read the old correspondence to understand the matter and then brief counsel to prepare them for hearing. Every day, I was dying bit by bit under the weight of the monotony and rigour. This was the second biggest setback to my career, and I had no idea when the turmoil would end, and when my career would take off in the true sense.

I was on the verge of giving up on my dream of becoming a corporate lawyer. With great reluctance, I even forced myself to apply at Godrej Soaps for the post of legal manager. During the interview, the incumbent legal manager, a wise man, patiently heard me out before advising me to practice some old-fashioned patience and continue with CB. He reckoned I must give CB some more time since it was a good law firm. Enthused by his comforting words, I decided to continue my litigation work at CB.

Within a year's time, I was rewarded for my patience. As soon as I knew of a vacancy at Mr. Shah's Chambers, I switched over without a second thought and Mr. Shah also readily accepted me. And mind you, during those days shifting from one Partner to another was not an easy task! This transfer marked the turning point of my career. Working with Mr. Shah was an awesome experience. Even today, at this juncture of my career, I would give an arm and a leg to work as his junior: attending client meetings, taking instructions from him, discussing different law propositions, conducting research and analyzing legal propositions, preparing notes for his speeches, and simply observing him at work: his phenomenal patience, excellent listening skills and polite expression at any meeting. His drafting style – whether for letters or opinions – was simple, precise, and purposeful. He was always respectful towards everyone; always positive, proactive, and polite in all conversations. The individuals he interacted with comprised the Who's Who of law and business including Nani Palkhiwala, Ratan Tata, Nusli Wadia, Ajay Piramal, K. K. Modi and many luminaries from abroad. As a highly competent lawyer, he had the uncanny ability to gauge the crux of the subject matter within no time, and also offer a 50,000-foot view for the benefit of the given audience. His ability to stay objective and probe the root of any issue was incredible! Needless to say, he was extraordinarily brilliant in finding the most amicable solution, a win-win for all concerned parties. He was, and is, the Trusted Advisor of choice for many industrialists, professionals, and decision-makers!

6.7   Metro Work culture defined by Retro-style communication

Today's generation thriving on Microsoft Teams, Zoom, and Google Meet cannot ever imagine the sedate work environments of the nineties. Today, people find it hard to believe that the mobile phone was a distant dream until 1996. Hence, I deem it fit to give a glimpse of the interaction and communication, the way we did it way back then.

In Crawford Bayley, the best mode of communication with foreign clients was telex. By the end of 1991, facsimile via telephone arrived on the scene and we happily switched over to the regime of the prized fax machine! I recollect the first fax I sent to the Legal Department of Steel Authority of India

(Calcutta) intimating them about the High Court hearing of their matter. I was accustomed to sending voluminous JV documents, continuously editing them and resending them via fax. We had to make photocopies of the entire fax as the ink faded after some time. And if that was not enough, we got daily calls from the General Post Office (GPO) in Mumbai to check whether we used our telephone line for faxing documents.

The first true revolution in document management happened with the advent of Windows 95. Though it was not Microsoft's first-ever operating system based on a graphical user interface, Windows 95 represented the biggest step away from the far less user-friendly MS-DOS system. This was a momentous period for Indian business and industry when the proliferating communication technologies coincided with the rapid growth in foreign collaborations. And my typing skills helped me gain quick mastery over the computer keyboard, which was a great help for preparing documentation.

6.8 Business value of Linguistic skills

As mentioned earlier, my knowledge and fluency of Kutchi (Gujarati) connected me deeply with many renowned Gujarati Businessmen in India including the Shahs (founders of Anchor) and Chudgars (founders of Intas Pharmaceuticals) besides senior finance professionals and chartered accountants like Shailesh Haribhakti, Gautam Doshi, Bansi Mehta, and Arun Gandhi. How I wish I had learnt the German language back in the 1990s when I started working with Mr. Shah in Crawford Bayley. Somehow, Germany has been a key focus geography for me, given esteemed clients like Bayer, BASF, Siemens, Fresenius Kabi, Hannover Re, and many others. I would like to strongly recommend young lawyers or other consultants working with international companies to learn at least one foreign language, be it German, French or Japanese. Knowing the language of a given country opens its business doors in unimaginable ways, bestowing a phenomenally huge advantage!

6.9 The Big Leap of Liberalization

In July 1991, the then Finance Minister of India Dr. Manmohan Singh announced the new industrial policy which allowed foreign ownership in 34 industries to be raised to 51% from 40%. The Narasimha Rao government also allowed licensing of technology to Indian companies under the automatic route. This decisive step marked the beginning of a new era for Indian corporates. Mr. Shah was on the board of around 60 multinational companies (MNCs), primarily advising them on how they should raise their ownership stakes in India in the new Foreign Direct Investment (FDI) regime. Consequently, companies like Coca-Cola (and PepsiCo) returned to India in 1993.

It may be recalled that Coca-Cola was the leading soft drink brand in India until 1977 when it left India after the government ordered the company to dilute its stake in its Indian unit. It is pertinent to note that the government had earlier forced foreign companies to reduce their ownership to 40% under the Foreign Exchange Regulation Act, 1973 (FERA). At that time, the abysmally low foreign exchange reserves of the country were a scarce commodity. Later, under Dr. Singh's Economic Liberalization initiative, the Government replaced FERA with the liberal Foreign Exchange Management Act, 1999 (FEMA) which allowed the increase of ownership up to 51%, and even 100% in some select industries.

From 1992 to 1999, I represented the crème de la crème of Fortune 500 and top-notch companies under the visionary guidance of Mr. Shah. Our clientele included heavyweights like Colgate, Proctor & Gamble, Bayer AG, BASF AG, Boots Plc, Beiersdorf AG, Scholl Plc, Gladerma, Unilever, Cadburys, Abbott, Fresenius Kabi, SmithKline Beecham, Amoco Corporation, Philip Morris, Roche, Rhone Poulenc, Allergan, Fiat, Seagram, Black & Decker, SKF, Akzo Nobel, Givaudan Roure, Guinness Plc, Standard Chartered, AIG, Tatas, Piramals, RPG, Asian Paints, Bombay Dyeing, Britannia, and Atul Ltd.

6.10 M&A deep dive

We worked on highly innovative and intricate M&A and JV deals of listed and unlisted companies. We regularly got esteemed references from the likes of Ashok Wadhwa (who was then managing partner at Arthur Andersen) and investment banking firms like Udayan Bose (Lazard), Nimish Kampani and Adi Patel from JM Financial, Kotak (JV with Goldman Sachs), DSP Merrill Lynch, and many small Indian and overseas boutique firms.

During this period, I touched the depths of Transaction tax and Valuation, two key drivers of any M&A deal, from seasoned chartered accountants like

Bansi Mehta, Arun Gandhi (NM Raiji & Co), Dilip Doshi (C.C. Choksi & Co), Y. H. Malegam (S.B. Billimoria & Co), N. V. Iyer, not to mention senior partners from big accounting firms like Arthur Andersen, Coopers & Lybrand, Deloitte & Touche, Ernst & Young, KPMG and Price Waterhouse. Every interaction was illuminating and inspiring in the same breath.

Being the blue-eyed boy of Mr. Shah, he assigned me key international matters without a second thought, such was his faith in me, and he invariably applauded my effort. I soaked in the wisdom of this farsighted leader, studying his remarkable flexibility of approach without compromising his core, and his success mantra for difficult situations – of negotiating, conceding, compromising, and then, crossing over. He was a thoroughbred professional and very strict about meeting deadlines and keeping his word. These were the most potent working tools that Mr. Shah gifted me on a platter.

Thanks to the strong working relationships, many of my clients now share a deep bond with me and consider me their trusted advisor. Notable among them were Ashok Chhabra and Deepak Acharya, both from Proctor & Gamble, K. V. Vaidyanathan of Colgate Palmolive India, M. R. Iyer of BASF, Gavaskar of Boots, Keval Handa of Abott, Madhav Joshi of Bayer, C. B. Gagarani of Century Enka (Birla Group), and N. Santhanam of Bombay Dyeing.

Most of my work during this period was about setting up joint ventures, technical collaborations, mergers & acquisitions, and demergers, as also business restructuring involving asset/business sale, succession planning, legal due diligence and advising on exchange control regulations and corporate advisory services to MNCs and their Indian affiliates and subsidiaries. We interacted directly with the key decision-makers: the board members and top management.

My first key M&A work under Mr. Shah was representing Colgate-Palmolive India Ltd in the $41.7 million acquisition of the oral hygiene business of Hindustan Ciba-Geigy, the Indian subsidiary of Ciba-Geigy A.G. of Switzerland (Ciba-Geigy). Hindustan Ciba-Geigy was 40 per cent owned by Ciba-Geigy. Under the purchase agreement, Colgate took over Cibaca toothpaste and other brands, as well as Ciba-Geigy's distribution and manufacturing arrangements. The purchase increased Colgate's share in India's toothbrush market to more than 70 per cent. It was a great learning experience working with the M&A Head of Colgate on how to structure the documentation for large and complex M&A transactions. His association gifted me with a treasure trove of invaluable insights. Mr. K. V. Vaidyanathan (Company Secretary & Legal Counsel of Colgate) was also extremely meticulous and equally supportive.

I was a regular visitor to the residence of the Chief Justice of India, Late Y. V. Chandrachud to seek his opinion on various corporate matters. I have lost count of the interesting courtroom stories I heard, straight from the horse's mouth. Those were the golden days of my early career. I fondly recall the excellent working relationship I had quickly established with the late Rashmi D. Chandrachud (wife of SC Judge Dhananjay Y. Chandrachud, son of Late Y V Chandrachud). She represented Ciba-Geigy under the supervision of her senior Late Mr. Jangoo Gagrat, Senior Partner of Gagrat & Co., another reputed law firm in Mumbai. Mr. Gagrat and Mr. Shah were the best of buddies although they belonged to rival law firms. They shared their views with each other without the slightest hesitation. At the same time, they duly respected their professional boundaries. Unfortunately, I don't see that happening today with young lawyers even from the same law schools.

I fondly recall the string of Tata group assignments on which I worked very closely with Mr. Shah. In one key assignment, he was consulted by the Tata senior management on the unique 'TATA Brand Equity & Business Promotion (BEBP) Agreement" as they call it now. Essentially, every company that uses the 'Tata' brand is a signatory to the Tata Sons' BEBP agreement. The agreement confers upon the operating companies the right to use the Tata brand in return for a commitment from them to run their businesses ethically and with excellence. Mr. Shah, during his early days in his career, had extensively worked on matters concerning intellectual property including trademarks, patents, copyrights and designs; he had a thorough knowledge and understanding of the tenets of global brands/goodwill and reputation. Following the Tata Brand agreement, many other Indian groups also executed similar agreements to protect their respective brands.

My association with the Tatas continued even after my CB tenure, both during the Amarchand Mangaldas (AM) stint and the current J. Sagar Associates (JSA) stint. Notable transactions in the AM stint included the massive legal due diligence of the entire operations of Tata Consultancy Services Ltd., for their maiden initial public offering. Incepted in 1968, TCS had grown into one of India's largest and most profitable companies with an annual revenue of more than $1 billion. One of the Wall Street Journal's headlines of the said time conveyed it all: Big IPO in India Could Trigger Market Revival. Later, in 2019, I worked closely with the senior management of TCS on the major reshuffle of key employees and other critical compliances.

I attended several professional meetings with Mr. Shah wherein there was a lot of learning – just to give a flavour – Once he was asked by a large American Bank to seek the opinion of Mr. Nani Palkhivala (one of the greatest intellectual jurists of modern India) on the predictability of certain tax provisions in India. Mr. Shah had personally prepared the written brief, which Mr. Palkhivala had read in advance and was ready with his detailed notes. For over an hour, he gave us an overall picture of where the tax regime in India was falling short of international expectations, and what could be done to overcome that impediment. As a law student at Government Law College, I regularly attended Mr. Palkhivala's annual lectures on India's Union budget at the iconic Brabourne Stadium, Churchgate. However, the opportunity to be all ears to him in person, observing his humility and professionalism from close quarters, has been one of the biggest achievements of my professional career, which I will cherish all my life!

6.11   Paradigm shifts in the SEBI regime

The whole environment was electric as given the opening of the Indian economy, most foreign companies from the US and Europe sought to up their shareholding from 40% to 51% to acquire majority stakes in their Indian affiliates. This was the most opportune time for them to strengthen their market position by acquiring leading Indian companies and brands and consolidating their positions. The booming M&A market was at an all-time high.

On the one hand, the corporate landscape was changing rapidly, on the other, the Securities Exchange Board of India (SEBI) came into being, a watchdog to protect investor interest, promote the development of stock exchanges, and regulate stock market activities.

In 1994, SEBI came up with the first Takeover Regulations. Under Mr. Shah's guidance, I represented Bombay Dyeing, which had made a competitive open offer for the Ahmedabad Electric Company (AEC), in response to the voluntary open offer made by Torrent Group to acquire

AEC. This was the first-ever open takeover battle which severely exposed the SEBI Takeover regulations. SEBI was forced to set up the Justice Bhagwati Committee (Ex-Chief Justice of India) to review the Takeover provisions, and Mr. Shah was invited to join as the committee member.

Here again, I was fortunate to work closely and assist Mr. Shah in preparing the proposed amendments to the Takeover Code. SEBI had provided us with a lot of reading material including Australian and UK codes which I studied in great detail. During that evolutionary phase of SEBI Takeover regulations, we represented several companies who sought to defend against hostile bids from Asian Paints, Saurashtra Cements and the like.

Like Mr. Shah, I was invited as a guest speaker by esteemed bodies like the Institute of Company Secretaries, the Institute of Chartered Accountants, various Stock Exchanges, and Law Schools to unfold the essence of the SEBI Takeover Code, Joint Ventures and Foreign Collaboration and Mergers & Acquisitions.

In what was my first truly independent assignment, I represented the Indian subsidiary of the German chemicals and pharma giant Bayer AG, which made an open offer to acquire ABS Industries Ltd (a listed Indian company). This was the first time a foreign company made an open bid for an Indian firm following the enactment of the takeover code. This was a milestone deal as I had structured a first-ever and unique preferential allotment (primary issuance) of around 31% equity shares to Bayer and a balance of 20% via an open offer, which was the mandatory size of an open offer under the SEBI Takeover Regulations.

The Indian corporate world was thereby introduced to a novel structure for acquiring a listed company through a combination of issuance of fresh shares followed by an open offer from the public. As preferential allotment was exempt from the SEBI Takeover Regulations, the very acquisition of a 31% stake rules out or frustrates the possibility of any competitive bid. I thoroughly relished working hand in hand with the M&A team of Bayer AG at Leverkusen, Germany.

Mr. Shah proudly acknowledged my contribution to designing this mode of acquisition. That was a watershed moment for me, for I had won accolades from the master for my professional acumen. In fact, in an informal chat, the then SEBI Chairman told Mr. Shah that this process was against the spirit of the SEBI Takeover as it stifled the possibility of competing bids.

For Bayer AG, this acquisition was extremely important because ABS Industries was making acrylonitrile butadiene styrene, an engineering plastic used in various industries like automobiles, consumer electronics, and the luggage segment. Bayer has worldwide operations in acrylonitrile butadiene styrene, but none in India. This acquisition won Bayer a dominant share of the ABS market without investing heavily in a greenfield plant, a grand entry into India blessed with an enviable edge. What more could have Bayer asked for?

Based on the same strategy of issuance of fresh shares, we helped a family-owned cement company successfully defend a hostile bid. This was followed by a string of similar deals shielding companies against many a hostile bid.

6.12 Joint Ventures deep dive

The most popular investment theme for the Western world at that time (1991 onwards) was 'Destination India'. Every foreign company wanted to set up a joint venture or technical collaboration in India. On the other hand, many Indian entrepreneurs who visited the US or Europe hastily signed MoUs for setting up JVs in India. The majority of these MoUs were open-ended and allowed foreign companies to hold 51% equity ownership, precisely because the foreign companies aimed at consolidation and dominant control given their superior technology and brand power.

However, over time, even 50:50 JVs were signed with one extra director to the foreign collaborator to enable consolidation. Consequently, many friendly JVs came into being. Where any conflict arose, the foreign players were ready for a compromise as they were eager to commence business in the goldmine that India was.

For me, the most interesting part of the negotiations was the provisions with regard to buy-out clauses in the case of deadlocks, 50:50 shareholding, or an exhaustive list of items requiring affirmative votes. Deliberating with Mr. Shah on the alternative structures to resolve conflicts or deadlocks proved a highly interactive and fascinating learning. Mr. Shah had a lot of insights into the workings of the Indian companies, their succession planning, and management styles. He was thus able to quickly recommend tailored mechanisms for deadlock resolution. Among these options, Russian Roulette was my favourite.

That structuring a Joint Venture is more a business decision than legal is something I learnt under the tutelage of Mr. Shah. We must have together structured over 100 JVs and multiple other forms of alliances for Indian and Foreign Companies operating in India. I had the complete freedom to suggest equity, management structure, and deadlock resolutions. I distinctly recollect our representation on behalf of a large Indian Hospital run by a very senior US-retuned doctor. He was negotiating with a Private Equity (PE) investor to acquire a stake in his hospital. The PE investor had a veto on all critical items save for one. I had proposed that in the event of a deadlock, the founder doctor should have the first right to offer to purchase and/or replace the PE investor at the 'fair price' decided by any independent valuer. My logic was rooted in the fact that the hospital was essentially an Indian venture. However, the PE fund manager stridently sought the right to counter and out-bid. Mr. Shah intervened on behalf of the Founder Doctor and made it abundantly clear that if the proposal were not acceptable, he would find another investor who would allow the Founder Doctor to cherish his dream of serving his home country. Such was Mr. Shah's conviction that the PE Investor finally gave his consent to the deadlock resolution.

Whilst discussing the basic structure of equity of 50:50 or 51:49 or any minority investment, Mr. Shah spent substantial time understanding the ownership structure, role of founders, their managerial capability, role of strategic partners, tentative business plan for the next five to ten years, and the way competitive businesses were positioned. He would counsel the founders to keep their expectations at reasonable levels. Because of his vast experience of working with MNCs operating in India, he knew how decisions were usually made and proceeded with. At the same time, he was very closely associated with the Indian founders. He never advised any client to take advantage of any situation and was always fair, objective, and reasonable in recommending a prudent business decision without compromising on commercial interest of both parties.

In what was an interesting case, two brothers of a large electronic goods company and liquor were fighting tooth and nail over ownership issues. We were representing the elder brother who was extremely furious, keen on kicking his younger brother out of business as the latter was siphoning funds.

Mr. Shah intervened and convinced him to make an amicable separation and thereby, avoid bitter court battles, which would only be in the interest of lawyers from a purely financial perspective.

Inevitably, the Indian owners were averse to negotiation (or even discussion) on deadlock resolution clauses. In sharp contrast, the foreign companies were always open to a detailed deadlock resolution mechanism including the final buy-out provisions. We had to spend considerable time explaining to the Indian promoters that it is in their interest to have clarity on the way forward lest things do not materialize or if partners do not get along well. I recall a JV finalization between a large Indian house and an MNC where the company chairman explicitly told us to keep the matter open and not provide any solution. Why? Because he was nervous about something going wrong even before the JV was signed.

6.13   Dizzying Career Highs

It was normal to provide that following the termination of the JV Agreement, the party existing should not compete with the JV nor poach the key employees of the company. The big question was about the validity of such non-compete provisions particularly when the joint venture is in the form of a company. Lawyers were divided on this issue and the majority were of the view that this restrictive provision was against section 27 of the Indian Contract Act, 1872, which declared that any agreement that restrains anyone from exercising a lawful profession or trade or business of any kind, is to that extent void.

I did some research on this topic and argued that under section 36(2) of the Indian Partnership Act, 1932 it is legally permissible to restrict an outgoing partner from carrying on any business similar to that of the firm within a specified period or local limits, and this is notwithstanding anything contained in Section 27 of the Indian Contract Act, 1872. I relied on the jurisprudence of our Supreme Court which in several of its leading cases declared that joint ventures are quasi-partnerships, and it is permissible to apply the principles of partnership for dissolution in such joint ventures. My opinion was widely circulated in corporate circles and accepted by a majority of corporate lawyers whilst structuring joint ventures. (Refer to the Supreme Court implications in the landmark judgment of Gujarat Bottling Case cited in the chapter on Joint Ventures.)

One of my key representations, in the liberalization era, was Fiat SpA which had identified a huge potential in the Indian car market. I went to the Turin headquarters of Fiat in December 1996 at the behest of Mr. Scognamilio, the then General Counsel to prepare and negotiate the technical collaboration with Premier Automobiles Limited (PAL). As part of Fiat's World Car Project for emerging markets, the Fiat Uno vehicle was imported and assembled from completely-knocked-down (CKD) kits. Simultaneously, Fiat set up its wholly owned greenfield plant at Ranjangaon near Pune in Maharashtra for the production of its World Car model range.

This was the time when Maruti Suzuki had no competition in India. Maitreya Doshi, the Managing Director of PAL, was keen to develop a car to compete with Maruti, what with Hyundai already having announced its plans to set up a small car manufacturing plant in Chennai.

I also worked with a large Indian Pharma group which got big during the 90s merely on the strength of a series of strategic M&As. The chairman had built quite a reputation for managing successful JVs with MNCs. His instructions to me were very clear: in case of any difference of opinion or dispute, let parties bid for each other's shares after determining the minimum fair valuation decided by any independent agency. The whole idea was focused on protecting the interests of the JV Company, not the individual shareholders.

6.14   The AM sojourn: My tryst with a Family-owned setup

Sometime in 1997, CB decided to add around six new partners (Prem Rajani, Sanjay Ashar, Sujjain Talwar, Marco Wadia, and myself) and I consider myself fortunate to be named in the probable list. However, for reasons best known to the then partners of CB, we were not made partners despite announcing the date for our induction. We were all terribly disappointed and I had almost decided to quit the firm, when all of a sudden, I got a call from Cyril Shroff to join his law firm Amarchand Mangaldas & Suresh A. Shroff & Co. (as it was known prior to their split between Cyril Shroff (Mumbai) and Shardul Shroff (Delhi). Even from the first meeting, I struck a chord with Cyril and decided to join him. As an Amarchand Mangaldas (AM) partner, I continued my M&A work with the same vigour as before.

AM had been advised by external consultants to broaden their partnership and that is how I was identified by Cyril to join the firm. I must say that AM, though a family-owned firm, was totally committed to the goal of making the firm truly international in size and substance. Cyril was criticized for his autocratic functioning to which he had a matter-of-fact reply, "I am a benevolent dictator, and I do not want my firm to become a debating society."

Cyril was clear about the need to make quick decisions in the larger interest of the firm. I enjoyed an extremely cordial working relationship with Cyril and Shardul and their respective wives Vandana (an astute lawyer who maintains a firm grip over the admin support of AM Mumbai Office) and Pallavi (a Delhi-based litigation and competition lawyer, and daughter of Former Chief Justice of India P. N. Bhagwati), as also their mother late Bharti Shroff (herself a banking and finance lawyer). In 2014, almost nine years after I had left them, the family entity was split following the demise of Bharti Shroff. Now both Cyril and Shardul successfully run their own firms and have grown even bigger individually.

I was advised by many colleagues against joining AM in 2000 because it was a family-owned and run firm, but I took a conscious call to join them. I had decided to give myself five years with AM but actually clocked in a year more. I have no regrets about having given six years to AM as I had the freedom to run my M&A practice. Yes, had Cyril entrusted me with more responsibility, I would have probably stayed longer. I was keen to be part of the development process, particularly the IT infrastructure or Knowledge Management of the firm. But since both of them were hands-on in business development and management, there was hardly any role for an outsider, and rightly so.

The most important part of business development, where you meet with senior partners of international firms or the management team of top clients, was handled by Cyril and Shardul almost exclusively for the reasons best known to them. I guess they wanted their teams to focus on execution and believed that good work would automatically fetch good business. That apart, there is a lot to learn from both Cyril and Shardul. They both are well-respected and well-networked names in the Indian corporate world. I am not aware of their working style post the split but would always remain their well-wisher and cherish those days.

My notable transactions in the AM stint included the massive legal due diligence of the entire operations of Tata Consultancy Services Ltd (as mentioned above). Following the success of the TCS IPO, I conducted the legal due diligence of Ultra Tech Cement - the Cement Division of India's largest engineering conglomerate, Larsen and Toubro Ltd (L&T), which was sold to the Aditya Birla Group.

Among other interesting cases during the AM tenure was the demerger and separation of the listed player Duphar Interfran from Solvay Pharmaceutical Ltd. I extensively worked with Vishal Nevatia, Managing Partner of Truth North Fund (earlier known as India Value Fund), a homegrown private equity firm. I advised Sharavan Shroff of Shringar Films (the largest film distributor in India) on their foray into the multiplex business in Mumbai. I also relished working with Gautam Saigal of AIG Global Investment Group (Asia) and Co-Head of India PE advisory practice.

6.15   The JSA chapter: Pinnacle of my M&A and JV Voyage

AM was essentially a family-owned firm, so in due course, I sought opportunities to work with a more egalitarian setup. I joined J. Sagar Associates (JSA) in October 2005, and I resigned in June 2024 (3 years ahead of my retirement) to pursue my passion of mentoring young law students/ professionals. A truly merit-based and democratic law firm, JSA is structured just like any European or American law firm. It has an elected managing committee, and it offers partners complete freedom for practice based on mutual trust. The uniqueness of our firm is that we, by constitution, have agreed not to take any of our family members on board, only to steer clear of any bias, and we also have a compulsory retirement age of 65. In fact, Jyoti and Berjis retired at 60! And the next generation of leaders has successfully transitioned into playing bigger roles. We have a fantastic battery of young promising lawyers who I am sure will do exceedingly well in their respective practice areas and take JSA to new heights.

I have continued my M&A and Foreign investment work with even more enthusiasm in the JSA era. My work includes business restructuring, asset/ share transfer deals, private equity, business succession planning, and general corporate advisory. I have built a team of good lawyers besides contributing to the growing list of esteemed clients. Somehow, my focus has remained on working for German companies like Fresenius Kabi AG, which I have serviced for over 15 years, including serving as an independent director on their Indian-listed subsidiary. Transitioning to JSA was easy for me as I had worked with the chairman Jyoti Sagar in 1996 when I represented French Magazine ELLE and

Jyoti represented Bhartia Group. I found Jyoti extremely polite and cordial during that interaction and this experience had actually sowed the seeds in my mind, of considering JSA as a prospective firm to partner with. In another coincidence, my first transaction as a Partner of AM was against Berjis Desai (JSA Managing Partner Mumbai) wherein I stood for AIG Fund for a private equity investment in a French Company Ethypharm represented by Berjis. In the very first interaction, I had won the faith and trust of Berjis who gave me a free hand to negotiate on the investment documents.

The leadership of Jyoti and Berjis was accommodative, democratic, and respectful. They insisted we partners be always open and collaborative. In turn, all partners have strived to maintain the DNA of our firm, built brick by brick by Jyoti and Berjis. When I joined JSA in 2005, the firm had a total of 63 lawyers across three locations. Today in 2023, we are a big family of 450 professionals and 7 offices - a perfect blend of senior and junior partners - spread across seven locations, including the office I started at GIFT IFSC, Ahmedabad in 2018 for a specific duration.

In all humility, I feel elated to mention that I have worked on many landmark and marquee transactions in the Indian Corporate world. It would be pertinent to take a closer look at a couple of them, as well as a few of the key litigations handled by me.

6.16 Anchor – Panasonic

Anchor Electricals, the 50-year-old family-owned top-notch brand was sold to Matsushita Electric Works (maker of Panasonic Japan's No 1 brand in electric equipment) for 50 billion yen ($420 million). I found the deal extremely interesting as I represented the entire family that owned Anchor and closely worked with them for almost nine months. I conducted a time-consuming and backbreaking vendor legal diligence of the entire Anchor operations prior to the negotiations and documentation. This effort was necessary because of the vast operations of Anchor spread across India which had to be consolidated from multiple smaller firms into one entity for ensuring ease of transfer. I am glad that Atul Shah, the Managing Director of Anchor, reposed total confidence in me to handle negotiations, documentation, and closure end to end. My Kutchi language proficiency again played a key role in strengthening the relationship as the Shah family belongs to the Kutchi Community.

Knowing their mother tongue made our conversations as seamless as possible. During the negotiations, I worked closely with the legal counsel David Allen Tally and several team members from Panasonic. The Panasonic team was extremely meticulous in its approach and the whole environment was very cordial and harmonious.

As a matter of practice, whenever I deal with a reputed brand, I study a little bit of its history, in particular the groundwork done by the founders. When I did extensive research on Panasonic and studied their past acquisitions across the globe, I was more than confident that they would go all out to acquire Anchor, the number 1 brand in India. Also, during informal conversations with their team, I sensed their deep aspiration to assume a numero uno position in any country. I subtly unfolded the Anchor success story for their benefit, how they became a trusted household name in India. This elaboration helped iron out many minor issues and eased the negotiations. I thoroughly enjoyed representing Atul Shah and his family members, and they continue to be my clients to this day.

6.17 Camlin-Kokuyo

I represented the founding family of Camlin No. 1 in stationery products in India when they sold their controlling stake to Kokuyo No. 1 in paper products in Japan. The acquisition was structured as a combination of 10 per cent shares via primary issue, an open offer for 20 per cent as mandated under the SEBI Takeover Regulations, and around 20 per cent from the founders. Exiting the business was an extremely emotional decision for the family. Hence, I had structured the management transition in a phased manner which allowed the Dandekar family to cherish their position and reputation as one of India's leading brand makers. Fortunately, the family reposed total confidence and faith in me for the negotiations that took place in Tokyo. My objective was to tick mark all the minimal but decisive commercial points towards ensuring an amicable agreement. Thanks to my studied approach and grasp of the subject matter, I stayed focused, assertive, and firm in my position end to end. And since I was singlehandedly leading the negotiations, I had to act extremely tough on behalf of my client, which created an image, in the minds of the Kokuyo management, that I was an extremely aggressive lawyer. Having said that, during the concluding phase of negotiations, the Kokuyo management team wholeheartedly appreciated the steadfast manner in which I represented the Dandekar family. Right from the beginning, I was convinced about the certainty of this deal. Camlin did enjoy an enviable reputation in India as a stationery giant, but since the market was becoming ultra-competitive, I was confident that Kokuyo would offer best-in-class support to Camlin – whether in terms of raw material quality, best-of-breed equipment, R & D capabilities, or the financial muscle to infuse fresh capital.

6.18   2011 Tokyo earthquake

After three days of hectic negotiations in Tokyo, I stayed back to meet a few reputed law firms in Tokyo. On my last day in Tokyo, Friday 11th March 2011, I was in a meeting with Mr. Ushijima, the founder of a local law firm Ushijima & Partners. At 1.45 p.m., Japan (Pacific Coast) was hit by an earthquake of magnitude 9.0–9.1. Mr. Ushijima's secretary, visibly shaken, entered our conference room and conveyed the news. I was on the 12th floor of Sanno Park Tower, and the lights went out. From the balcony, I recorded a short video on my mobile capturing the shuddering building and people running helter-skelter on the streets. Mr. Ushijima asked me if I was fine! I told him, "If you are fine, I am fine!" Anyway, after an hour or so, I had to climb down 12 floors to begin a one-hour walk to my hotel.

I later learnt about the horrifying enormity of the disaster. It was an undersea megathrust earthquake off the coast of Japan with an epicentre of approximately 70 kilometres east of the Oshika Peninsula of Tōkyo. Aptly called the Great East Japan Earthquake, or the 2011 Tōkyo earthquake, it was the most powerful earthquake ever recorded in Japan, and the fourth most powerful earthquake in the world since the advent of modern record-keeping in 1900.

I was astonished to note the patience and discipline that common people demonstrated on the streets of Tokyo. There were no metros, buses, or taxis plying on the road; people were quietly walking on the footpaths without the slightest anxiety or hassle. Since I had no clue of the directions, I had to frequently consult pedestrians. Many of them had small maps of Tokyo with them and were very proactive in helping me find my way back. With my return flight having been cancelled, I called home and informed my wife about my safety. I was in compulsory confinement in my hotel room for the next three days, watching and admiring Japan systematically responding to the disaster. People patiently queued up for water bottles and food packets. I came back to Mumbai with a successful deal and an earth-shattering experience of a lifetime…literally!

6.19   LIC Nominee Directors on L&T Board – Corporate Litigation

Whilst all my life I have practised as a Corporate Lawyer, I have also worked as a litigation lawyer for high-profile matters. I distinctly remember that LIC (Life Insurance Corporation of India – India's state-owned largest personal insurance group and investment corporation) sought my advice on their corporate governance issues, particularly about their nominee directors on the boards of various LIC-invested companies. It had all begun with a Business Standard headline about two nominee directors of LIC having received employee stock options from Larsen & Toubro Limited (L&T), the well-known Indian conglomerate into technology, engineering, construction, manufacturing, and financial services that was founded by two Danish engineers. The stock options so granted were clearly in violation of the letter and spirit of the employee stock option regulations applicable for listed companies. Essentially, to be eligible for getting employee stock options shares, one must be in regular employment and not merely a nominee director of an investor, like LIC in this case.

LIC wanted to act against their own nominee directors, and my friend, Ms. Sadhna Dhamne, the Legal Counsel of LIC, approached me and asked me to take appropriate action. I immediately consulted Sr. Counsel Ravi Kadam of the Bombay High Court, and we moved the Court to seek an injunction against the two nominee directors. I called up the Editor of Business Standard and informed him about the injunction order; the news was also widely reported by many other newspapers. Embarrassed by the media attention, the two nominee directors of LIC were all too keen to settle the matter amicably, which did happen soon after.

6.20   MCX-SX Stock Exchange

In another major corporate litigation, I represented MCX-SX, the equity Stock Exchange in India set up by my client Jignesh Shah (who was named the Global Young Leader by the World Economic Forum in 2007).

Somehow, the Securities and Exchange Board of India, the regulator of the securities and commodity market in India, was not in favour of granting permission to MCX-SX to open a full-fledged Equity Stock Exchange that would compete with the Bombay Stock Exchange and the National Stock Exchange of India. It was apparent the action of SEBI was patently wrong. We had to fight an extremely bitter court battle which went right up to the Supreme Court.

I also worked extensively for the Jignesh Shah-promoted Financial Technologies (FTIL) (now known as 63 Moons Technologies Limited) which offers technology intellectual property to create and trade on financial markets. I helped FTIL set up and divest various exchanges globally including Dubai, Singapore, and Mauritius.

6.21 GIFT IFSC

I worked extensively with the Management of GIFT IFSC for the Gujarat International Finance Tec (GIFT) City, Ahmedabad. GIFT City is India's first operational smart city and international financial services centre, comparable with financial centres in Dubai, Singapore, London and Dublin. The integrated development covering 886 acres of land with 62 mn sq. ft. of Built-Up area includes Office spaces, Residential Apartments, Schools, Hospitals, Hotels, Clubs, Retail and various Recreational facilities, which makes this City a truly "Walk to Work" City. GIFT City consist of a conducive Multi-Service SEZ (Special Economic Zone) and an exclusive Domestic Area.

I had the opportunity of working closely with Ajay Pandey, Managing Director, and Dipesh Shah, Head - Development and International Relations to structure various legislations including the 50 key amendments to the Indian Companies Act, 2013 that offered certain special exemptions and benefits to companies set up in GIFT IFSC. Separately, I was instrumental in successfully setting up a collaboration between GIFT IFSC and the Singapore International Arbitration Centre (SIAC) and also helped GIFT IFSC in structuring the establishment of the International Financial Services Centres Authority, 2019 to regulate all financial services in GIFT IFSC. This unified authority would be headquartered in Gandhinagar, Gujarat providing a single-window regulatory institution to accelerate the development of India's first IFSC.

Prior to the inception of this unified regulatory authority, the Banking, Capital markets, and Insurance sector regulations in GIFT IFSC were being done by multiple agencies, namely the Reserve Bank of India (RBI), Securities and Exchange Board of India (SEBI), and the Insurance Regulatory and Development Authority of India (IRDAI) respectively.

6.22   Addendum to my Corporate Work
Book on Entrepreneurship

My mainstream career took an unexpected turn with the completion of the landmark Anchor-Panasonic transaction (mentioned above). After the press conference, I was interviewed by the business correspondent of 'Loksatta' (a Marathi newspaper of the Indian Express group) Mr. Prasad Kerker on my role as a corporate lawyer in mega deals, India's foreign investment policies, and the trends of foreign investment in India. He insisted that I write about my experiences on Joint Ventures and Foreign Collaborations and various aspects of Entrepreneurship. Pursuant to his request, I wrote around 20 articles between 2007-2010 on Entrepreneurship, Capital, Innovations, Foreign Collaborations, Human resources, Marketing, Branding, and Trends. At the behest of Shri Kumar Ketkar (Senior Editor), I compiled these articles and published a book titled 'Pragaticha Expressway' on 16th February 2011. Soon after, in addition to my regular lectures on M&As and JVs for law students, I started sharing my experiences at various business forums, chambers and management schools.

6.23   MAXELL FOUNDATION (Maharashtra Corporate
Excellence Awards)

During these sessions, I realized that entrepreneurship education and encouragement hold the key for the next generation. Encouraged by the reception of my book and responses to my business sessions, I incepted Maxell Foundation (www.maxellfoundation.org), a non-profit trust (2012-2017) conferring the Maharashtra Corporate Excellence Awards for felicitating and encouraging entrepreneurs, innovators, business leaders, and young startups from the State of Maharashtra. The advisory board comprised the who's who across diverse sectors: Dr. Raghunath Mashelkar (India's Premier Scientist),

Kumar Ketkar (Sr. Editor), Late Y. M Deosthalee (Chairman & CEO of L&T Finance), Justice (Retd.) Arvind Savant, Sunil Deshmukh (Renowned Commodity Trading Expert), Shailesh Haribhakti (Sr. Chartered Accountant), and Dinesh Keskar (Sr. VP Boeing India). From 2012 to 2017, we conferred around 42 Maxell Corporate Excellence Awards to achievers across diverse sectors and spheres in grand annual ceremonies at landmark venues.

6.24 MAXPLORE – Teaching Entrepreneurship in Schools

Meanwhile, I designed a short program titled 'Maxplore' for teaching entrepreneurship to school and college students wherein I shared the concept of '3-i Introspect, Ideate and Implement'. I published a short practical guide to develop entrepreneurial traits amongst school children which was published at the hands of Shri Rahul Bajaj (senior industrialist) at the Maxell Annual Awards - 2016. I personally took a few pilot sessions on entrepreneurship for school and college students in Mumbai and Pune. It is still a work in progress! Sam Pitroda (father of India's Computer and IT Revolution) was the Chief Guest for the Maxell Awards in 2017, who suggested that I do 'conversations' in lieu of the awards functions. I deliberated on his suggestion with my advisory board and we terminated the Maxell Awards in 2017.

6.25 INDIA POWER TALK

However, the idea of holding conversations stayed in my mind. Almost three years later, when the pandemic enforced a lockdown in March 2020, the concept and craze of 'Zoom' digital meetings had caught on. On the economic front, rightly or wrongly, while China faced a backlash from the international community for the spread of Covid 19, India caught the attention of global companies as an alternate manufacturing destination. I swung into action and set up the 'India Power Talk' (www.indiapowertalk.com) – a digital platform (webinar series) assembling international leaders from diverse sectors to talk about the economy, environment, and education. The idea is to create an easily accessible digital source of diverse business knowledge, which would benefit Indian entrepreneurs, internatonal businesses, institutional investors, and strategic partners, either active in India or intending to invest in the country. Indian Chamber of Commerce, Indo-American Chamber, and LawSikho (the largest online education company) came forward to share their members as the audience. I am happy that, in a span of 10 months, I have hosted around 16 distinguished guests who have shared their thoughts with me on various interesting subjects.

The journey continues...

Key representations over the years by Nitin Potdar	
Nissan Distribution (in their restructuring Indian operations)	Monash University, Australia
Clearwater Capital Fund	TOTAL SA France
Kinetic Engineering	NTT Data Corporation, Japan
Cookie Man Australia for India entry	Resolution plc and Friends Provident plc (in their global merger having an impact in India)
Pantaloon (Future Group) in their series of JVs including Dixons UK, LeeCooper UK, Liberty Shoes, ETAM, Future Capital	Tamasek Singapore
Robeco Group N.V., Netherlands (for setting up JV with Canara Bank)	T-Systems Enterprise Business Services GmbH
Alteams Oy for setting up JV in India	(subsidiary of Deutsche Telekom AG)
Devgen NV, Belgium	Springer Science + Business Media, Germany
Ecom Agro-industrial Corp Ltd	Swiss Re, Switzerland
Associated British Foods Plc	Vertellus Specialities, US
IFCI Ltd	Cementia Trading AG, Zurich
Ecocert SA, France	Ecolab Inc, US
FMO (the Netherlands Development Finance Company)	Enics Group, Zurich
HTC Sweden AB	Hitachi Automotive, Germany
Paracor Capital Advisors	Knorr-Bermse, Germany
Sportal Australia Pty. Ltd	Petronas, Malaysia
Bayer HealthCare AG	Fori Automation, US
BP Energy	Nissan Japan
Maxis Communications, Malaysia	Titan Cement Company S.A
Nisshinbo, Japan	Altana AG, Germany
OFIC Onduline, France	Grundfos AG
General Mills Inc, US	The Timken Company Inc, US
Hannover Re, Germany	CDI Corporation Inc., US
Interserve Plc, UK	Sony Corporation US
	DKSH
	LIC India
	Wockhardt Ltd, India

Chapter 7

What Makes Us Successful and Happy

"It isn't where you came from; it's where you're going that counts."

- Ella Fitzgerald

To all aspiring law students and young lawyers,

The first and foremost important thing you should bear in mind is what Ella Fitzgerald has said, 'It isn't where you came from; it's where you're going that counts.' I would request you all to please read the inspiring story of Ella 'From Homeless to Household Name'. The majority of you may be not just thinking but almost convinced that law students who don't have a family background or some god-father cannot succeed. Please remove this misconception from your mind and stop getting disillusioned. There are literally thousands of top lawyers in India and across the globe who were all first-generation lawyers and enviably successful.

The keys to success and happiness are two-fold: (a) Being positive about our efforts in life and (b) Maintaining good relationships. As you embark on the demanding journey of becoming a lawyer, remember the power of being positive about your efforts. They are not just words, but seeds that, when planted in the fertile soil of your mind, can grow into unshakeable confidence and resilience. Embracing the unknown is a part of our legal journey starting from law school, as we navigate through uncharted roadmaps, unforeseen challenges, and an uncertain future, much like the diverse array of people we meet along the way, each with their unique stories and destinies. Amidst this rigour, it's crucial to remind yourself of your capabilities and potential. Making positive affirmations is your personal cheerleader, nudging you forward when doubts cloud your path. They help you foster a mindset of growth and perseverance, essential for navigating the intricate labyrinth of law. **Embrace affirmations like 'I am capable', 'I am learning', and 'I am growing stronger with each challenge'.** Let these words be your anchor in turbulent times, helping you stay grounded in your purpose and vision. Remember, the journey to becoming a successful lawyer is not just about accumulating knowledge, but also about building a resilient, positive mindset that can withstand the pressures of the legal world. So, affirm your strengths, believe in your journey, and watch as you transform challenges into stepping stones for success. Globally positive affirmations are considered a highly effective way of progressing, and in fact, there are several books, podcasts and YouTube videos on positive affirmations and actions. I would strongly recommend you to read those books and material.

The second important aspect is maintaining healthy relationships. Throughout my career, I have always placed immense value on maintaining good relationships. This personal commitment has taught me that in the legal profession, the skill of nurturing connections is as crucial as legal expertise. Strong, respectful relationships with colleagues, clients, and mentors are not just professional assets; they are the foundation upon which successful careers are built. These bonds not only expand our professional networks but also open doors to new opportunities and collaborations. **In a field where trust and reputation hold significant weight, the effort put into these relationships can profoundly influence the trajectory of our careers. By prioritizing these connections, we not only enrich our own professional paths but also contribute to a more supportive and dynamic legal community.**

I'd like to highlight a profound insight from Harvard's longest study on adult development, led by Robert Waldinger, the fourth director of the program. The study reveals that the key to a happy, healthy life lies in the quality of our relationships. This finding serves as a gentle reminder that, amidst the demands of the legal profession and the pursuit of success, nurturing our connections with others is not just important, it's essential. Life is not a mere race to be won but a journey to be cherished. The bonds we create and sustain are what truly enrich this journey. As you build your career, remember to also cultivate and treasure relationships based on respect, care, humility, integrity, and love. This includes everyone from your family - parents and siblings, no matter the circumstances - to your law school teachers/faculty, close friends, colleagues, mentors, clients, and all those who have supported, guided, and illuminated your path.

I must also share my own experience of working in law firms. I consider myself the most fortunate corporate lawyer for having worked with Crawford Bayley & Co (9 years), Amarchand Mangaldas (6 years before they split into CAM and SAM), and finally, J. Sagar Associates (18 years running) – please see the detailed work I did in my journey given below. The working cultures of all these three firms were different and challenging at times. Yet, engaging and satisfying. When we work in larger organizations, it is possible that all your suggestions and actions may not get approved and at times, you may not get the credit for what is rightfully due to you. **I remember the famous quote from Henry Ford who said, "Coming together is the beginning. Keeping together is progress. Working together is success."** The most important skill for success is to have people on your side. One can get a lot of work done by superiority and hierarchy, but one cannot be a leader of men unless one maintains excellent human relationships. And success depends upon how good you are at maintaining relationships.

You may ask me how to maintain relationships with those who seem hostile or navigate unfavourable/challenging circumstances. A simple solution lies in maintaining a stance of empathy and understanding. It's important to remember that hostility often stems from underlying issues or misunderstandings. Approach these situations with patience and an open mind. Seek to understand their perspective and communicate your thoughts and feelings calmly. Follow what Bernard Meltzer had said 'Before you speak ask yourself, if what you are going to say is true, is kind, is necessary, is helpful.' If the answer is no, maybe what you are about to say should be left unsaid. This approach not only helps in de-escalating potential conflicts but also paves the way for building mutual respect and understanding. Remember, every difficult interaction is an opportunity to learn and grow, both personally and professionally.

For your convenience and deeper understanding, I have included below key excerpts from the insightful TED Talk given by Robert Waldinger on January 8, 2016, which eloquently encapsulates the essence of this significant study.

What makes a Good Life?

BY ROBERT WALDINGER
Fourth Director of The Harvard Study of Adult Development
Excerpts from his TED Talk, Jan 08, 2016

What keeps us healthy and happy as we go through life? If you were going to invest now in your future best self, where would you put your time and your energy? There was a recent survey of millennials, asking them what their most important life goals were, and over 80 per cent said that a major life goal for them was to get rich. And another 50 per cent of those same young adults said that another major life goal was to become famous.

And we're constantly told to lean into work, to push harder, and achieve more. We're given the impression that these are the things that we need to go after in order to have a good life. Pictures of entire lives, of the choices that people make and how those choices work out for them, those pictures are almost impossible to get. Most of what we know about human life is from asking people to remember the past, and as we know, hindsight is anything but 20/20. We forget vast amounts of what happens to us in life, and sometimes, memory is downright creative.

But what if we could watch entire lives as they unfold through time? What if we could study people from the time that they were teenagers all the way into old age to see what really keeps people happy and healthy?
We did that. The Harvard Study of Adult Development started in 1938, may be the longest study of adult life that's ever been done. For 75 years, we've tracked the lives of 724 men, year after year, asking about their work, their home lives, their health, and of course, asking all along the way without knowing how their life stories were going to turn out.

Studies like this are exceedingly rare. Almost all projects of this kind fall apart within a decade because too many people drop out of the study, funding for the research dries up, or the researchers get distracted, or they die, and nobody moves the ball further down the field. But through a combination of luck and the persistence of several generations of researchers, this study has survived. About 60 of our original 724 men are still alive, still participating in the study, most of them in their 90s. And we are now beginning to study the more than 2,000 children of these men. And I'm the fourth director of the study.

Since 1938, we've tracked the lives of two groups of men. The first group started in the study when they were sophomores at Harvard College. They all finished college during World War II, and then most went off to serve in the war. And the second group that we've followed was a group of boys from Boston's poorest neighbourhoods, boys who were chosen for the study specifically because they were from some of the most troubled and disadvantaged families in the Boston of the 1930s. Most lived in tenements, many without hot and cold running water.

When they entered the study, all of these teenagers were interviewed. They were given medical exams. We went to their homes and we interviewed their parents. And then, these teenagers grew up into adults who entered all walks of life. They became factory workers and lawyers and bricklayers and doctors, one President of the United States. Some developed alcoholism. A few developed schizophrenia. Some climbed the social ladder from the bottom all the way to the very top, and some made that journey in the opposite direction.

The founders of this study would, never in their wildest dreams, have imagined that I would be standing here today, 75 years later, telling you that the study still continues. Every two years, our patient and dedicated research staff calls up our men and asks them if we can send them yet one more set of questions about their lives.

Many of the inner-city Boston men ask us, "Why do you keep wanting to study me? My life just isn't that interesting." The Harvard men never ask that question.

To get the clearest picture of these lives, we don't just send them questionnaires. We interview them in their living rooms. We get their medical records from their doctors. We draw their blood, we scan their brains, and we talk to their children. We videotape them talking with their wives about their deepest concerns. And when, about a decade ago, we finally asked the wives if they would join us as members of the study, many of the women said, "You know, it's about time."

So, what have we learned? What are the lessons that come from the tens of thousands of pages of information that we've generated in these lives? Well, the lessons aren't about wealth or fame or working harder and harder. The clearest message that we get from this 75-year study is this: Good relationships keep us happier and healthier. Period.

We've learned three big lessons about relationships. **The first is that social connections are really good for us, and that loneliness kills.** It turns out that people who are more socially connected to family, to friends, to community, are happier, they're physically healthier, and they live longer than people who are less well connected. And the experience of loneliness turns out to be toxic. People who are more isolated than they want to be from others find that they are less happy, their health declines earlier in midlife, their brain functioning declines sooner and they live shorter lives than people who are not lonely. And the sad fact is that at any given time, more than one in five Americans will report that they're lonely.

And we know that you can be lonely in a crowd, and you can be lonely in a marriage, so **the second big lesson that we learned is that it's not just the number of friends you have, and it's not whether or not you're in a committed relationship, but it's the quality of your close relationships that matters.** It turns out that living in the midst of conflict is really bad for our health. High-conflict marriages, for example, without much affection, turn out to be very bad for our health, perhaps worse than getting divorced. And living in the midst of good, warm relationships is protective.

Once we had followed our men all the way into their 80s, we wanted to look back at them at midlife and see if we could predict who was going to grow into a happy, healthy octogenarian and who wasn't. And when we gathered together everything we knew about them at age 50, it wasn't their middle-age cholesterol levels that predicted how they were going to grow old. It was how satisfied they were in their relationship. The people who were the most satisfied in their relationships at age 50 were the healthiest at age 80. And good, close relationships seem to buffer us from some of the slings and arrows of getting old. Our most happily partnered men and women reported, in their 80s, that on the days when they had more physical pain, their mood stayed just as happy. But the people who were in unhappy relationships, on the days when they reported more physical pain, it was magnified by more emotional pain.

And the third big lesson that we learned about relationships and our health is that good relationships don't just protect our bodies, they protect our brains. It turns out that being in a securely attached relationship to another person in your 80s is protective, that the people who are in relationships where they really feel they can count on the other person in times of need, those people's memories stay sharper longer. And the people in relationships where they feel they really can't count on the other one, those are the people who experience earlier memory decline. And those good relationships, they don't have to be smooth all the time. Some of our octogenarian couples could bicker with each other day in and day out, but as long as they felt that they could really count on the other when the going got tough, those arguments didn't take a toll on their memories.

So, this message, that good, close relationships are good for our health and well-being, this is wisdom that's as old as the hills. Why is this so hard to get and so easy to ignore? Well, we're human. What we'd really like is a quick fix, something we can get that'll make our lives good and keep them that way. Relationships are messy and they're complicated. The hard work of tending to family and friends is not sexy or glamorous. It's also lifelong. It never ends. The people in our 75-year study who were the happiest in retirement were the people who had actively worked to replace workmates with new playmates. Just like the millennials in that recent survey, many of our men when they were starting out as young adults really believed that fame and wealth and high achievement were what they needed to go after to have a good life. But over and over, over these 75 years, our study has shown that the people who fared the best were the people who leaned into relationships, with family, with friends, and with community.

So, what about you? Let's say you're 25, or you're 40, or you're 60. What might leaning into relationships even look like?

Well, the possibilities are practically endless. It might be something as simple as replacing screen time with people time or livening up a stale relationship by doing something new together, long walks or date nights, or reaching out to that family member whom you haven't spoken to in years because those all-too-common family feuds take a terrible toll on the people who hold the grudges.

I'd like to close with a quote from Mark Twain. More than a century ago, he was looking back on his life and he wrote this, "There isn't time, so brief is life, for bickerings, apologies, heartburnings, callings to account. There is only time for loving, and but an instant, so to speak, for that."

The good life is built with good relationships.

Thank you.

Robert

Chapter 8

Frequently Asked Questions

8.1 Law Profession

1. How can I be sure that a career in law is a good choice for me?
NP: Deciding on a career in law can be a major life decision, and it is important to carefully consider whether it is the right choice for you. The following are a few points to determine whether you can choose to have a career in law:

- Consider your interests

- Assess your skills!

- Research the legal profession

- Evaluate your career goals

- Consider the cost and time commitment

Having a career in law may not be everyone's cup of tea. Apart from the skills mentioned above, there are many other factors to consider before choosing your field of career such as your family background, your upbringing, the type of personality you have, etc. All these factors contribute to deciding whether you can become a successful lawyer and which field of law would suit you the best.

I have seen many students quitting law after the first/second year of their law course. I would strongly recommend that students opt for career counselling at least once in order to make the right decision.

(For further details, kindly refer to Chapter I point 1.4: Do an honest assessment of yourself, point 1.5: Appear for multiple aptitude tests, and point 1.6: Career counselling.)

2. What are the benefits of choosing law as a career?

NP: Choosing law as a career can offer a range of benefits, including:

- Intellectual Stimulation
- Career Opportunities
- Financial Reward
- Influence and Impact
- Personal and Professional Development

Overall, choosing law as a career can be a fulfilling and rewarding choice for those who are passionate about justice and enjoy intellectual challenges. However, before choosing law or for that matter, any career option, I would strongly recommend undergoing an aptitude test or consulting a good career counsellor. I have elaborated on this aspect in the main book; please refer to the same.

3. Which qualities must I have before taking admission to law?

NP: The majority of Indian students, when considering their future careers, often bypass crucial steps like aptitude tests or career counselling. This oversight can lead to choosing a profession that may not align with their inherent skills and interests. In the context of pursuing a career in law, this can be particularly significant. Law is a demanding field that requires a specific set of qualities for success.

Ideally, individuals considering law should possess **strong analytical and communication skills, ethical integrity, and resilience.** They should be adept at research, have an eye for detail, and be **capable problem solvers**. Empathy, emotional intelligence, and a passion for justice are also key. Effective time management, adaptability, teamwork, critical thinking, and public speaking skills round out the essential qualities. Additionally, an ongoing interest in learning is vital due to the ever-evolving nature of legal work.

Understanding and matching these qualities with one's personal attributes is crucial. Aptitude tests and career counselling can play a significant role in this process, helping prospective law students make informed decisions about their suitability for a career in law.

(For further details, kindly refer to Chapter I point 1.3: Practice of law)

4. Is LL.B. more difficult than other professional courses?

NP: It is difficult to compare LL.B. with other professional courses as the level of difficulty can vary depending on the individual's background, interests, and aptitude. That being said, LL.B. is a challenging course that requires a high level of commitment, hard work, and dedication.

LL.B. courses typically involve a lot of reading, research, and writing, as well as critical thinking, analysis, and interpretation of legal concepts and principles. Students are also expected to develop strong communication and advocacy skills, as well as the ability to work well under pressure.

One of the main challenges of studying law is the volume and complexity of legal materials that must be mastered, including case law, statutes, and legal treatises. Additionally, the study of law requires a significant amount of time and effort outside of the classroom, including research, writing, and preparation for moot court and other legal competitions.

5. I have a very quiet/introverted personality. Can I still have a future in law?

NP: Yes, having a quiet or introverted personality does not necessarily mean that you cannot have a successful career in law. While some aspects of the legal profession may require more extroverted qualities such as public speaking, networking, and negotiation, there are also many roles in the legal field that may be better suited for introverted individuals.

For example, research-oriented roles such as legal research, writing, and analysis may be well-suited to those with introverted personalities.

It is important to note that while being introverted may present certain challenges in the legal field, it is not necessarily a disadvantage. Many successful lawyers and legal professionals are introverted and have found ways to leverage their strengths to excel in their careers.

6. The admission procedure is too complicated. Are there any institutes that help with the process?

NP: Yes, there are several institutes in India that help students with the admission process for law schools. These institutes offer guidance and counselling services to help students navigate the complex admission procedures and increase their chances of getting admitted to their desired law schools.

Some of the popular institutes that provide such services include Career Launcher, T.I.M.E., IMS Learning Resources, and Endeavor Careers. These institutes offer coaching classes, study materials, mock tests, and other resources to help students prepare for the law entrance exams and improve their chances of success.

7. Which qualities would I master if I take admission in law?

NP: Studying law can help you develop a range of valuable qualities and skills, including:

- Critical Thinking
- Problem-Solving
- Research Skills
- Communication Skills
- Attention to Detail
- Time Management
- Professionalism

Overall, studying law can help you develop many qualities that are highly sought after in many different professions.

(For further details, kindly refer to Chapter III point 3.15: Core skills and experience)

8.2   Before Taking Admissions in any Law School

8.   What are the eligibility criteria to get admission to a law school?

NP: The eligibility criteria for admission to law school in India can vary depending on the institution and the program you're applying to.

For Undergraduate Law Programs (LLB):

- **Educational Qualification**: Candidates must have completed their higher secondary education or an equivalent examination with a minimum of 45-50% marks (depending on the institution).

- **Age limit**: There is no upper age limit for admission to most law schools in India. However, some institutions may have an age limit for admission to the LLB program.

- **Entrance Exam**: Most law schools in India require candidates to take an entrance exam, such as the Common Law Admission Test (CLAT), All India Law Entrance Test (AILET), or State-level law entrance exams.

For Postgraduate Law Programs (LLM):

- **Educational Qualification**: Candidates must have completed an undergraduate law degree (LLB or equivalent) with a minimum of 50% marks.

- **Entrance Exam**: Some law schools in India may require candidates to take an entrance exam, while others may offer admission based on merit or previous academic performance.

9.   Which law program is better? 5-year or 3-year?

NP: In general, a 5-year law program, such as an integrated law program or a law program with a year of legal practice, provides a more comprehensive and specialized legal education than a 3-year program. Technically, there is no difference, but the 5-year program may sound more advantageous because you then spend more focused time pursuing law right from the beginning.

On the other hand, a 3-year law program also provides you the required legal education but may be more suitable if you are interested in a career in general legal practice or if you are looking to complete your legal education more quickly. Graduation is required to be eligible for a 3-year law course.

It is also important to consider factors such as the reputation of the law school, the quality of the faculty and curriculum, and the availability of internships and other practical learning opportunities when choosing between a 5-year and 3-year law program.

10. What are the criteria for selecting a Law School?

NP: The criteria for selecting a college can vary depending on your personal goals, preferences, and circumstances. If I have to enlist a few general factors to consider, they will be as follows:

- Academic Programs

- Location

- Size

- Cost of education

- Campus Life

- Reputation

- Diversity and Inclusivity

It is important to prioritize what factors are most important to you when selecting a college and to research and visit multiple colleges to get a better sense of which one is the best fit for you.

(For further details, kindly refer to Chapter II: Roadmap to enter legal profession)

11. What are the benefits of attending a reputed law school?

NP: The benefits of attending a reputed law college over a mediocre college are as follows:

- **High-Quality Education:** Reputed law colleges generally offer a high-quality education, with experienced faculty, comprehensive curriculums, and access to advanced resources and technologies. This can provide students with a solid foundation in legal theory and practice, and better prepare them for success in their legal careers.

- **Better Career Opportunities:** Graduating from a reputed law college can provide students with better career opportunities, as top law firms and employers often prefer to hire graduates from well-regarded institutions. Additionally, reputed law colleges may have stronger networks and connections to the legal industry, which can help students secure internships, clerkships, and other professional opportunities.

- **Prestige and Reputation**: Attending a reputed law college can also provide students with a sense of prestige and reputation, which can be beneficial in building their professional networks and gaining recognition within the legal community.

- **Access to Resources and Support**: Reputed law colleges often provide students with access to a wide range of resources and support services, such as career services, academic advising, and student organizations. These resources can help students succeed academically and professionally and provide valuable opportunities for networking and personal growth.

While gaining admission to a prestigious law school can undoubtedly set the stage for a successful career, it's crucial to remember that the true determinant of success in the legal field lies in your personal dedication and effort. Prestigious institutions provide valuable resources and networks, but they are merely a foundation. The real work begins with your individual commitment to hard work, your ability to think critically and creatively, and your drive to make a distinctive mark in the legal community. Success in law is not just about where you study, but how you leverage your education, cultivate your skills, and carve out your unique path in the vast and competitive world of law.

12. How much does it cost to attend a law school?

NP: The cost of attending law school in India can vary depending on the type of institution, location, and other factors. Fees of NLUs and private colleges can be a little expensive, but a student can opt for various aids available for students with limited means. Also, Government Colleges and Government aided colleges have a much more economical fee structure than other colleges.

College brochures are available on the websites of colleges with the exact structure of their respective fees. These brochures are updated every year.

(For further details, kindly refer to Chapter II point 2.5: Cost/benefit analysis and job market realities)

13. What is the difference between the curriculum of colleges like (a) National Universities like NLUs, (b) Private colleges like O.P. Jindal, NMIMS, Symbiosis, etc. (c) other colleges affiliated to Mumbai University like GLC, KC? More importantly, how can I decide which will be a good fit for me?

NP: The curriculum of colleges in the field of law can vary depending on the type of institution.

- **National Universities (NLUs):** NLUs are established by the central or state government and are considered to be premier institutions for legal education in India. The curriculum in NLUs focuses on a comprehensive study of law, including core subjects like contracts, criminal law, constitutional law, and more specialized subjects like international law, intellectual property law, and human rights law. NLUs also provide a strong foundation in legal research, writing, and advocacy skills.

- **Private Colleges:** Private colleges like O.P. Jindal, NMIMS, Symbiosis, and others typically have a more flexible curriculum that can be tailored to the needs and interests of the students. These colleges often offer a wider range of elective courses, including courses in emerging areas of law, and may place greater emphasis on practical skills like legal drafting, client counselling, and negotiation.

- **Other colleges affiliated with Mumbai University like GLC, KC:** These colleges typically offer a more traditional curriculum that covers core legal subjects and emphasizes foundational skills like legal reasoning, research, and writing. The curriculum may be less flexible than that of private colleges, but students may have more opportunities to gain practical experience through internships and other experiential learning opportunities.

To decide which type of institution would be a good fit for you, it is important to consider your career goals and learning preferences. National Universities may be a good fit if you are interested in pursuing a career in academia or in highly specialized areas of Law, while private colleges may be a good fit if you are interested in a more hands-on, practical approach to legal education. Other colleges affiliated with Mumbai University may be a good fit if you prefer a more traditional, foundational approach to legal education.

Please refer to the websites of the above-mentioned law schools for better understanding.

14. Which type of college should I opt for if I want to practice only in my native village?

NP: If you are interested in practising law in your native village in India, it may be beneficial to choose a college that is located in or near your village or in a nearby city. This can help you develop local connections and gain knowledge of the local laws and legal practices.

However, it is important to choose a college that provides a strong foundation in law and legal skills, regardless of its location.

When choosing a college, you may want to consider factors such as the quality of the faculty, the availability of experiential learning opportunities like internships and clinics, and the reputation of the institution. It may also be helpful to speak with current students and alumni of the institutions you are considering to get a better sense of their experiences and the opportunities available to them.

Answering this question also made me wonder about the struggles of students coming from smaller villages to pursue law in urban cities. The transition from a small village to an urban city to pursue law can be a difficult one for students, but with the right support and determination, they can overcome these challenges and succeed in their studies.

15. Do I need to do any prerequisite courses before taking admission in a law school?

NP: In India, there are no specific prerequisite courses required to be completed before admission to a law school. However, having a strong foundation in certain subjects may be helpful in preparing for the law school curriculum. These subjects include:

- English
- Social Sciences
- Legal Studies
- General knowledge

While these subjects are not mandatory prerequisites, having a strong foundation in them can help you succeed in law school and in your career as a lawyer. It's also important to note that law schools may have different admission requirements and may value different areas of expertise. So, it's important to check the specific admission requirements of the law schools you're interested in applying to.

(For further details, kindly refer to Chapter III point 3.13: Pre-law classes)

16. Is coaching necessary for the preparation of entrance exams?

NP: Coaching for law entrance exams can be helpful for some students, but it is not necessarily required. The decision to take coaching or prepare on your own will depend on your individual learning style, study habits, and level of motivation. It is understandable that opting for coaching may not be a practical option for everyone.

Coaching can provide a structured approach to studying and may offer personalized guidance on areas of weakness. Experienced faculty members can provide valuable insights into the exam pattern, question types, and exam strategies.

Self-preparation can also be effective, especially if you are disciplined, organized, and can maintain a consistent study schedule. You can use a variety of study materials, such as textbooks, online resources, and previous year question papers, to prepare for the exam.

17. Does it matter how many times I take the entrance exam?

NP: In India, law entrance exams are conducted annually for admission to undergraduate and postgraduate law programs. Candidates are allowed to take the exam multiple times, and the highest score is usually considered for admission.

While taking the exam multiple times may not be a negative factor, it's important to note that the competition for admission to law schools in India can be intense. Therefore, it's essential to prepare thoroughly and perform well on the exam to increase your chances of admission.

It's important to check the specific admission requirements of the law schools you're interested in applying to and prepare thoroughly for the exam to maximize your chances of success.

18. I have never liked reading and studying, but I find litigation fascinating. Can I have a good future in litigation?

NP: While reading and studying are important components of a career in law, it is possible to have a successful career in litigation without necessarily enjoying those aspects of the profession. However, it is important to keep in mind that litigation involves a significant amount of research and preparation, writing, analytical skills, and strong oratory skills are necessary to be effective in this area of practice.

That being said, if you find litigation fascinating and are willing to put in the work required to succeed, there may be a future for you in this field. You can focus on developing your skills in research, writing, and analysis, which are essential for effective litigation practice.

Practising in the fields of litigation, arbitration, and alternative dispute resolution (ADR) in India offers not only the potential for substantial remuneration but also immense personal and professional satisfaction. This is particularly true given the vast backlog of cases that Indian courts are currently facing. For legal practitioners, this scenario presents a rich landscape of opportunities to engage in diverse and challenging cases. The high demand for skilled professionals in these areas means that lawyers with expertise in litigation, arbitration, and ADR can find themselves in a rewarding position, both financially and in terms of the impact they can make. Helping clients navigate through complex legal disputes and contributing to the resolution of long-standing cases not only brings financial rewards but also the profound satisfaction of facilitating justice and contributing to the efficiency of the legal system.

19. How can I do my undergraduate in law abroad? Does it make sense to study law abroad?

NP: If you're interested in pursuing an undergraduate degree in law abroad, here are some steps you can take:

- **Research Law Schools**: Start by researching law schools in the country you're interested in studying. Look for programs that align with your interests and career goals. Check the admission requirements, tuition fees, and scholarships available.

- **Check Eligibility**: Check the eligibility criteria for admission to law programs in the country you're interested in studying.

- **Apply for Admission**: Once you've identified the law schools, you're interested in applying to, submit your application for admission. The application process may vary depending on the institution, so be sure to follow the instructions carefully and submit all required documents.

Studying law abroad can be a rewarding experience, but it requires careful planning and preparation. Be sure to research your options thoroughly and seek guidance from the appropriate authorities to ensure a smooth transition.

Nowadays, students seem to think that the education system in other countries is better than that of India. I have a strong opinion that it is not necessary to go abroad searching for good quality education when institutes like NLUs and many other colleges are just as good. In fact, if you are planning to practice in India, then studying in India would be a better choice in order to understand the laws and practical background of law in India.

(For further details, kindly refer to Chapter V point 5.8: Paradigm shift-foreign universities and local profession in India)

20. I have done my graduation in a completely different field from law, but I find law interesting. Will I be able to become a successful lawyer?

NP: Yes, it is possible to become a successful lawyer even if you have done your graduation in a completely different field from law. Many successful lawyers have backgrounds in diverse fields such as engineering, medicine, finance, and humanities.

To become a successful lawyer, it's important to have a strong foundation in legal concepts and principles. You can gain this knowledge by pursuing a law degree or by enrolling in a diploma or certificate course in law. Some law schools also offer part-time or online courses that can be pursued alongside your current job or studies.

(For further details, kindly refer to Chapter I point 1.3: Practice of law)

21. Can I have a career in law after doing Engineering?

NP: Yes, as I explained in the previous question, it is very much possible to have a successful career in law after completing any degree. Many law schools welcome applicants with diverse educational backgrounds, and some law firms actively seek out candidates with technical or scientific expertise. It is just that you may need a couple of years more before you start practising. In fact, we in India are hell-bent on putting our careers into a strict mental timeline. In my opinion, even if you take some time exploring, reskilling or even start pursuing a totally new career in your 20s right up to your 30s or even thereafter, it should not matter because you just don't want to drag your life into a career which doesn't make you happy. I have seen many medical students doing an MBA and have reached the pinnacle in a totally different industry.

If you are interested in pursuing a career in law after completing your engineering degree, consider researching law schools that offer joint degree programs in engineering and law. These programs typically allow you to earn both degrees in a shorter period than if you pursued them separately.

Alternatively, you can pursue a traditional law degree (LL.B.) and focus your legal studies on areas that relate to your engineering background. You can also look for law firms or legal departments that specialize in engineering or technology-related matters.

While an engineering degree may not be a typical path to a career in law, it can provide a unique set of skills and experiences that can be valuable in the legal field.

(For further details, kindly refer to Chapter I point 1.3: Practice of law)

22. I tried reading a few legal documents, but I wasn't able to understand a single sentence, now I am tensed about if I will become a good lawyer.

NP: It's natural to feel overwhelmed when reading legal documents or reported decisions from the High Courts or the Supreme Court for the first time, as legal language can be complex and difficult to understand. However, with time and practice, you can develop the skills and knowledge needed to read and understand legal documents.

To start, you can try breaking down the document into smaller parts and focusing on understanding each section individually. You can also look up legal terms and concepts that you are unfamiliar with to help you better understand the document as a whole.

It is rightly said that practice makes a man perfect. The more you read legal documents and become acquainted with the language, the better you'll be able to understand them correctly.

Becoming a successful lawyer takes time and practice, and it's important to be patient and persistent in your efforts. By continuing to work hard and develop your skills, you can overcome any initial challenges and become a confident and competent legal professional.

8.3   Questions Faced in Law School

23. Do my College Scores matter in the long run?

NP: Yes, your college scores in law school can matter in the long run, as they can impact your career opportunities and advancement within the legal profession.

Firstly, your grades in law school can impact your ability to secure internships, clerkships, and other job opportunities during and after law school. Employers often look at law school grades as an indicator of a candidate's academic ability, work ethic, and potential for success in the legal profession.

In addition, students with high grades may have an advantage when it comes to salary negotiations and career advancement.

Furthermore, your law school grades can also impact your ability to pursue further education and training in the legal field.

(For further details, kindly refer to Chapter III: Life in Law School)

24. Does it matter if I have failed for a year during my course?

NP: I failed in my first-year law (1988), then again in the second year (1990) and three times whilst appearing for my Solicitors Exam (1989-91).

Firstly, failing a year may impact your academic progress and may result in delayed graduation. This can affect your ability to secure job opportunities, internships, and clerkships during and after law school, as employers may prefer candidates who have graduated on time.

However, it is important to remember that failing a year does not define your entire legal education or career. Many successful lawyers have faced academic challenges during their education, but they were able to overcome them and still have a successful career in law.

If you have failed a year during your law course, it is important to reflect on what went wrong and make a plan to address any academic or personal issues that may have contributed to your setback. This could involve seeking academic support, counselling, or other resources that can help you improve your academic performance and mental health.

25. If I don't get admission into a good college, what can I do during the course of my degree to cope with students from reputed colleges?

NP: If you don't get admission into a good law college, don't worry. Firstly, not all from the top law schools have made big careers! Cool. You can still be highly successful in your career if you are willing to work hard and take the necessary steps to improve your knowledge and skills. Here are some tips that can help you cope with students from reputed colleges:

- **Work hard**: Hard work is the key to success in any field. Make sure you attend all the classes, complete all the assignments on time, and prepare well for exams.

- **Participate in co-curricular activities**: Participating in co-curricular activities such as moot court competitions, debates, and seminars can help you develop your skills and improve your knowledge of the law.

- **Develop your research skills**: Law is a research-oriented field, so it's essential to develop your research skills. You can start by reading books, legal journals, and law review articles.

- **Take online courses**: Online courses can be a great way to supplement your law degree. There are many websites such as Coursera, LedX, and Khan Academy that offer online courses on various legal topics.

- **Network**: Networking is an essential aspect of any career. Attend legal events, seminars, and conferences, and try to connect with legal professionals and experts in your field.

- **Internships**: Internships provide an excellent opportunity to gain practical experience and learn from experienced professionals. Try to intern at reputed law firms, corporate legal departments, or with senior advocates.

26. Is it a sensible choice to transfer to a better college halfway through pursuing my degree?

NP: Transferring to a better law college halfway through your degree could be (but not necessarily) a sensible choice if it aligns with your career goals and can provide you with better opportunities to achieve them. Before jumping to any conclusion, make sure you have discussed the pros and cons with someone senior in the profession or good alumni of the prospective college.

Here are some factors to consider before deciding:

- **Academic fit:** Before considering a transfer, make sure that the courses and curriculum offered by the new college are aligned with your academic interests and career goals.

- **Cost:** Consider the cost of transferring, including application fees, tuition fees, and living expenses.

- **Networking opportunities:** Check if the new college offers better networking opportunities through internships, moot court competitions, and other extracurricular activities.

- **Personal factors:** Consider personal factors such as location, quality of life, and support systems before planning to transfer.

27. How many hours of study should I put in every day to have a good knowledge in law?

NP: The number of hours of study needed to have a good knowledge in law may vary depending on the individual, the law school or program, and the specific courses being taken. However, as a general guideline, law students are typically advised to study for at least 3-4 hours per day or a total of 20-25 hours per week.

Moreover, while studying is an important part of gaining knowledge in law, it is also important to engage in other activities such as participating in moot courts, attending guest lectures, and networking with legal professionals to gain a well-rounded understanding of the legal profession.

28. How can I have an extra edge over my other classmates?

NP: Firstly, your competition should be with yourself only. See if you have improved from yesterday instead of comparing it with others because they would not be there after a few years.

(Kindly refer to Chapter III point 3.16: Follow SMART Mantra)

29. Apart from my law syllabus, what else can I read to enhance my legal knowledge?

NP: There are several valuable resources to broaden your understanding of the legal field in India. The more you read, the more your understanding will improve.

- Explore law subjects not covered in your coursework

- Read law reports

- Dive into law journals and legal publications

- Check out published books by successful lawyers in their specialized areas

- Read biographies and memoirs of Indian legal professionals

- Study classic Indian legal texts

- Stay informed with law-related news in newspapers and legal blogs

These materials provide a well-rounded perspective on legal matters in India and complement your law syllabus.

(For further details, kindly refer to Chapter III: Life in Law School)

30. Can I do parallel certificate courses in law with an LL.B.? Also, how helpful are they?

NP: Yes, you can do parallel certificate courses in law along with pursuing an LL.B. degree. However, you should ensure that the certificate courses are good and also recognized by the Bar Council of India or other relevant regulatory bodies.

Some popular certificate courses in law include Intellectual Property Law, Cyber Law, International Law, and Environmental Law, among others. However, you should ensure that the certificate courses you choose are aligned with your career goals and interests.

31. How can I understand a subject if we don't get a good professor in law college?

NP: If you find yourself without a strong professor in law college, there are still ways to understand the subject and excel in your studies. Consider these tips:

- Utilize online resources

- Attend seminars and workshops

- Read extensively

- Engage in discussions with classmates

- Seek guidance from a mentor

Remember, your success in law school ultimately depends on your dedication, hard work, and perseverance. Even without a top-notch professor, you can still achieve your academic goals by applying these strategies and putting in the effort.

(For further details, kindly refer to Chapter III: Life in Law School)

32. Is it fine if I don't take the moot court in college seriously if I want to become a corporate lawyer?

NP: Even if you want to become a corporate lawyer, it is important to take moot court seriously in college. Moot courts can help develop skills that are essential for any lawyer, including corporate lawyers.

- **Develops legal skills:** Participating in moot court competitions helps to develop various legal skills such as legal research, writing, and verbal argumentation (which is an extremely important skill).

- **Improves confidence:** Moot court competitions provide an opportunity to present arguments in front of judges and peers. This helps to improve confidence and public speaking skills.

- **Networking:** Moot court competitions provide an opportunity to network with peers, judges, and legal professionals.

- **Experience in litigation:** Even if you want to become a corporate lawyer, it is important to have a basic understanding of litigation.

In conclusion, moot court competitions are an important aspect of legal education and provide several benefits to law students, irrespective of their chosen field. It is recommended that you take moot court seriously and participate actively to gain the maximum benefit.

33. What are the benefits of writing research papers, moot court competitions, etc., in the long run?

NP: Writing research papers and participating in moot court competitions can offer several benefits in the long run. Most importantly, moot courts can certainly help build your confidence as a speaker when you enter the legal profession.

Here are some of the key advantages:

- Enhances research and analytical skills
- Improves legal reasoning
- Improves legal writing skills
- Builds confidence and public speaking skills
- Develops critical thinking
- Increases career opportunities

(For further details, kindly refer to Chapter III point 3.10: Writing research papers and point 3.11: Moot Courts should be made compulsory)

34. My father (or mother) is a practising advocate. Should I work for him/her or join some other office in order to gain more knowledge?

NP: Whether you should work for your father/mother or join another office to gain more knowledge depends on your personal and professional goals and choice. Working for your father/mother may provide you with a comfortable and familiar work environment, as well as the opportunity to learn from their experience and guidance. On the other hand, joining another office may expose you to different areas of law and different ways of practising law, as well as the opportunity to build your own network and reputation. Also, it would be a more professional and stricter atmosphere that would really help you grow independently.

Ultimately, both options can lead to a successful career in law. It's important to consider your own goals, interests, and values when deciding which path to take.

35. All my friends have background of lawyers in their families except me. I feel insecure about having a good future in law. Should I just quit?

NP: Contrary to the previous question, I have been asked this question by many students. Feeling insecure about your future in law because your friends have a legal background is understandable, but it shouldn't be a reason for you to quit. Here are some things to consider:

- **Your own abilities**: Your success in law school and as a lawyer depends largely on your own abilities, not your family background or the connections of your friends. If you are passionate about law and willing to work hard, you can still achieve your goals.

- **Diversity of perspectives**: Coming from a non-legal background can actually be an advantage in some ways, as you may bring unique perspectives and approaches to legal issues. Your background can also help you connect with clients who come from similar backgrounds.

- **Networking**: While your friends may have connections in the legal field, you can still build your own network through internships, networking events, and other opportunities. Don't be afraid to reach out to alumni or other professionals in the field for advice and guidance.

- **Support systems**: It's important to have a support system in law school and in your legal career, whether that's friends, family, or mentors. You can also seek out resources such as academic support services or career counselling to help you navigate any challenges you may face.

36. How important is it to have a good friend circle in law school?

NP: Having a good friend circle or close network in law school is extremely important and could be certainly beneficial in a number of ways.

Here are some reasons why:

- **Emotional support**: Law school can be challenging and stressful, so having friends who can offer emotional support and encouragement can make a big difference in your mental health and well-being.

- **Networking**: Your law school friends can become valuable networking contacts in the future, whether you're looking for a job or seeking advice on a legal issue.

- **Study partners**: Studying with a group can help you stay motivated and on track with your coursework, as well as provide opportunities for discussion and clarification of legal concepts.

- **Career development**: Your law school friends may end up working in a variety of legal fields, which can provide you with exposure to different areas of law and potential career paths.

Making friends in law school will be beneficial in the long run because you never know when you might need to approach your friends in high places!

(For further details, kindly refer to Chapter III point 3.1: Classroom attendance and study circles)

37. While studying law, on rethinking, I would not want to pursue a career as a practising lawyer.

NP: It is possible that you may not want to pursue your career as a practising lawyer as it is very demanding and highly competitive. Here, first I would strongly recommend you do a career or aptitude test and understand your strengths and weaknesses. And it is possible that whilst studying law, you may have liked it but later, you may have a different view. This is perfectly understandable. Once you have identified what your calling is, you may take up academic study of that subject and pursue your (For further details, kindly refer to Chapter I point 1.3: Practice of law) career. For example, you may want to become an ace photographer, or an author and do content writing, do digital marketing, you may be good at managing events, you may be good at any sport, and teaching is also not a bad idea. So, there are hundreds of career options in today's world of information technology. Life is a long journey and just spending 3 or 4 years studying law doesn't mean you have to become a lawyer and get stuck in it. Secondly, stop thinking about what people might say. Just remember it is your life and you should drive it as you wish! Period.

Do you know Engineers (IT, Chemical Automobile or any field) who study MBA and work in totally different industries and we call them successful? Then, why not a Law Graduate also become an MBA and run any organization? Or a Startup?

38. How important is it to create and maintain connections/contacts in law? And why?

NP: Creating and maintaining contacts and building your own network of good lawyers, company secretaries, chartered accountants, domain experts, consultants, and most importantly clients and friends in the legal profession is extremely important for several reasons:

a)   The legal industry is a referral-based business, and building a network of contacts can help you get new clients and business opportunities.

b)   Contacts can help you stay updated on the latest developments in your field, learn about job opportunities, and access resources and information that can help you improve your skills.

c)   Collaboration is essential in the legal profession. Contacts can help you find the right partners for collaborations on cases, projects, or research.

d)   Contacts can help you build your reputation in the legal industry.

e)   Contacts can help you advance your career by connecting you with mentors, advisors, and potential employers.

f)   Contacts can also provide you with valuable career advice and guidance.

39. How can I make and maintain useful contacts (Network) in law?

NP: Building and maintaining useful contacts (Network) is an important aspect of a successful career in law. In fact, I strongly believe that your Network is your true Net Worth! Please remember you cannot develop a good network overnight. Network doesn't get developed simply by collecting visiting cards or storing mobile numbers; more than simply meeting people having a meaningful conversation is important. And you need to have patience to yield results.

Here are some tips to help you <u>make introductions</u> to useful contacts:

- **Attend networking events:** Attend legal conferences, seminars, and other networking events to meet other legal professionals.

- **Join professional associations:** Join professional associations and organizations relevant to your field of interest.

- **Volunteer or intern:** Volunteering or interning with legal organizations is a great way to meet other legal professionals and gain practical experience.

- **Use social media**: Use LinkedIn to connect with other legal professionals and join relevant groups and discussions.

- **Follow up**: After meeting someone, follow up with them to maintain the relationship. This could be as simple as sending a thank-you email or inviting them to coffee.

- **Provide value**: When building and maintaining contacts, it's important to provide value. This could be by sharing industry news, offering to help with a project, or providing a referral.

It might be a little intimidating for students to approach successful lawyers, but it would be much more helpful if you prove your value first than just approaching them blankly.

8.4 Final year/after graduating

40. What are the best career options after a law degree?

NP: A law degree offers a wide range of career opportunities.

- **Advocate**: Advocates represent clients in courts of law and provide legal advice on various issues.

- **Corporate/General Counsel**: Corporate counsels work in-house for a company and provide legal advice on various issues such as contracts, employment law, intellectual property, litigation, and regulatory compliance.

- **Judicial Services**: A law degree is a prerequisite for judicial services. As a judge, you would preside over cases, make judgments, and ensure that the law is upheld.

- **Civil Services**: You can pursue a career in civil services and work in various government agencies, such as the Ministry of Law and Justice or the National Human Rights Commission.

- **Legal Analyst**: Legal analysts work in law firms, corporate legal departments, or consulting firms. They research and analyse legal issues to help lawyers prepare for cases, draft legal documents, and provide legal advice.

- **Legal Process Outsourcing**: Legal process outsourcing (LPO) firms provide legal support services to law firms and corporations. As an LPO professional, you would work on tasks such as document review, contract drafting, and legal research.

- **Academia**: You can also consider pursuing higher education and becoming a law professor. As a law professor, you would teach and research various legal subjects.

- **Legal Journalism**: If you have good writing skills, you can consider a career in legal journalism. As a legal journalist, you would cover legal issues, write about court proceedings, and analyse legal judgments.

41. How to find out which field in law is the most compatible option for me?

NP: Choosing a field of law can be a challenging task as there are various areas of law to specialize in, and each has its unique characteristics and requirements. Here are some steps that you can take to determine which field of law may be the most compatible option for you:

- **Identify your interests**: Consider the topics that you enjoyed studying in law school or any legal-related activities that you have enjoyed in the past. You may also want to consider the type of clients or cases that you would like to work with.

- **Consider your skills**: Assess your strengths and weaknesses to see which areas of law may be the best fit for your skillset. For example, if you are a strong communicator, you may want to consider litigation or negotiation-based fields of law.

- **Research different fields**: Spend time researching the different fields of law and their requirements. Talk to lawyers practising in different fields to gain insight into their work and daily activities.

- **Consider job opportunities**: Research the job market to see which fields are in demand and have the best job prospects. Consider the location of potential job opportunities, the work-life balance, and potential salaries.

42. What are the pros and cons of working in a law firm as opposed to working in a company as their in-house counsel?

NP: There is a big dilemma in the minds of young lawyers about these two options because a majority of law students aspire to be a reputed lawyer on his/her own merits; working as an in-house counsel is also being preferred these days, but I guess that's the second choice, which honestly, I don't agree. Internationally working as an in-house counsel or General Counsel is an excellent option.

It is only when we complete law that we realise the difference between the two, but everyone's first preference, I guess would always be to practice on his own as a lawyer! However, this is changing and young lawyers are increasingly opting for a full career as in-house counsel in the corporate world.

Working in a law firm and working as an in-house counsel for a company can offer different advantages and disadvantages. Here are some pros and cons to consider:

	Law Firm	Company
Pros	• Exposure to different practice areas • High-profile cases • Opportunity to specialize • Potential for higher earnings	• In-depth knowledge of any industry • Better work-life balance • More control over workload • Job security/good pay
Cons	• Demanding work environment • Limited work-life balance • Limited job security	• Could offer limited exposure to different practice areas • Less specialized work • Comparative low earnings potential

43. What is more beneficial, practising in any advocate's office or practising in a big law firm?

NP: Both, practicing in an advocate's office and a big law firm have their own benefits and drawbacks, and which one is more beneficial for you depends on your career goals and interests.

Practising in an advocate's office can provide you with a wide range of experiences and exposure to different areas of law, as well as the opportunity to work closely with clients. Also, two- or three-tier cities don't have big law firms. You may have the opportunity to handle your own cases and develop your legal skills at a faster pace.

On the other hand, practising in a big law firm can provide you with access to high-profile clients and cases, as well as the resources and support of a large organization. You may have the opportunity to work on complex cases and gain valuable experience in specialized areas of law.

Speaking for myself, I interned with a comparatively much smaller firm V. A. Phadke & Co., for my Solicitor's exam in Mumbai and later, joined Crawford Bayley & Co. I was fortunate that during my internship, I worked on property matters, and civil litigation (summary suits, suits for specific performance, winding up petitions and Court Schemes for M&A, conveyancing, and commercial contracts). We were also told to observe the Senior Counsel appearing in courts and I must say here that I was fortunate to listen to Fali Nariman, Soli Sorabjee, Jay Mehta, Virendra and Virag Tulzapurkar, Iqbal Chagla, Aspi Chinoy, Dr. D. Y. Chandrachud (Now CJI) (all form Original Side of the Bombay High Court); and Sr. Counsel Arvind Sawant, Bhimrao Naik, Ashok Tulpule from the Appellate Side.

44. How can I go about my placement after finishing law school?
NP: Please see Chapter IV: Entry into legal profession above.

45. Is it possible to change my department in the same law firm and shift to some other field of practice after a few years of post-qualification experience? E.g. litigation to corporate, civil to criminal, etc.
NP: Yes and no, as it depends upon the policy of the law firm. Many old law firms do not encourage or (like) juniors to change departments or even mentoring partners. But yes, it is possible to change your department and shift to some other field of practice after a few years of post-qualification experience. Many lawyers switch practice areas at some point in their careers for various reasons such as personal interest, job satisfaction, or better opportunities.

However, switching practice areas can be challenging and requires careful planning and preparation.

Here are some pointers that can help you transition to a new practice area:

a) Conduct extensive research about the practice area you want to switch to. Learn about the legal issues, procedures, and skills required for that practice area.

b)   Try to connect with lawyers and professionals in the practice area you want to switch to. Attend legal events, seminars, and conferences, and try to build relationships with experts in the field.

c)   Consider taking specialized courses or obtaining certifications in the new practice area. This can demonstrate your commitment to the new field and enhance your credentials.

d)   Consider finding a mentor who can guide you through the transition and provide you with valuable insights, advice, and support.

e)   Volunteering for pro-bono or community legal services in the new practice area can help you gain practical experience and develop your skills.

f)   Be prepared to start at a junior level and work your way up.

46. If I have finished my law degree, does that mean I will still have to keep reading various laws?

NP: Yes, as a practising lawyer, you will need to keep reading and staying updated on various laws and legal developments throughout your career. The legal profession is constantly evolving, and new laws, regulations, and legal precedents are established every year.

Staying informed about legal developments is not only essential for providing quality legal services to your clients but also for ensuring that you are complying with ethical and professional obligations. It is important to note that the legal profession requires ongoing learning and development to maintain your license to practice law.

47. Working hours in law are much more grinding than any other choice of career; how can I balance my personal life with such hectic days?

NP: Working in law firms can be demanding at times, and it's important to maintain a healthy work-life balance to avoid burnout and stress.

Here are some tips to help you balance your personal life with a hectic legal career:

- Make a to-do list of tasks you need to complete and prioritize them based on urgency and importance.

- Set boundaries between your work and personal life. Try to avoid working on weekends and after work hours unless it's absolutely necessary.

- Take regular breaks during the day to relax and recharge. Go for a walk, practice mindfulness, or listen to music to help you de-stress.

- Manage your time effectively by using tools like calendars and scheduling apps to keep track of your appointments and deadlines.

- **Most importantly, eat healthy food, exercise regularly, and get enough sleep to maintain good physical and mental health.**

- Consider seeking professional help if you're struggling with stress, anxiety, or burnout.

48. Being a lawyer will I always have extensive and exhaustive working hours than my friends who are not lawyers?

NP: Yes. As a practising lawyer, your working hours may often be more extensive and even exhaustive than those of your friends who are not lawyers. The legal profession is known for long working hours, high pressure, and tight deadlines, especially during critical stages of litigation or corporate transactions.

However, the working hours in the legal profession can vary widely depending on the type of law you practice, the size of the firm, the geographic location, and the nature of the work you are handling. For example, lawyers in small firms or solo practices may have more flexible working hours than those in large law firms or corporate legal departments.

Moreover, lawyers in some practice areas may have more predictable working hours than others. For instance, lawyers who work in government agencies, academic institutions, or in-house legal departments may have more regular working hours than those who practice litigation or work for a law firm.

49. Which is the highest-paid field in law?

NP: In India, the highest-paid law fields are typically in the corporate and commercial sectors, including corporate law, mergers and acquisitions, banking and finance, and intellectual property law. These areas of law are in high demand and require specialized knowledge and expertise, which command high salaries.

In addition, international law and arbitration, which involves resolving disputes between parties from different countries, are also high-paying fields in India.

50. How much salary should I expect being a fresher?

NP: The salary for a fresh law graduate can vary depending on several factors such as the law school you graduated from, the law firm or company you join, the location of the job, and the demand for lawyers in that field. On average, a fresher in law in Tier I Cities like Mumbai and Delhi can expect a starting salary of anywhere from Rs. 75,000/- up to 1,20,000/- and in Tier II Cities, from Rs. 20,000 onwards per month in India.

Competition in Tier I cities to get into big law firms is intense, and only a small percentage of law graduates can secure jobs in these firms.

It's important to note that salaries can vary significantly based on the field of law you choose and your performance on the job. As you gain experience and expertise in your chosen field, your salary can increase significantly over time.

51. Can I land a job in a Tier-1 law firm through a good reference?

NP: It all depends upon the reference and relationship with the law firm. While having a referral from someone within the firm can certainly help get your resume noticed, it is ultimately up to the law firm to decide who they want to hire based on a variety of factors, including your academic and professional qualifications, relevant experience, and interview performance. Internships through good references may be possible in Tier I firms but getting a job depends on your relationship with the firm.

It is important to note that while a referral can help open doors for you, it is ultimately up to you to prove yourself during the application and interview process. You will still need to demonstrate that you have the necessary skills, experience, and qualifications to succeed in a Tier-1 law firm environment.

It is like someone helping you quickly be on the racing line, but ultimately, you have to run the race on your own!

52. What are the pros and cons of working in a tier-1 law firm as opposed to working in a smaller firm?

NP: <u>Pros of working in a tier-1 law firm:</u>

- Reputation and prestige

- Networking opportunities

- High salaries and benefits

- Quality training and resources

<u>Cons of working in a tier-1 law firm:</u>

- Long working hours

- Competitive work environment

- Limited work-life balance

- Limited flexibility

Working in a smaller law firm can also have its advantages and disadvantages, such as greater flexibility and work-life balance, but less exposure to high-profile clients and cases. Ultimately, the decision between working in a tier-1 law firm versus a smaller firm will depend on your individual career goals, priorities, and preferences.

53. If I have a job in a smaller firm, will it make it impossible for me to later get into a tier-1 law firm?

NP: Not at all. Having a job in a smaller law firm does not necessarily make it impossible for you to later get into a tier-1 law firm. Many factors can influence your chances of getting into a tier-1 law firm.

To improve your chances of getting into a tier-1 law firm, you should focus on developing your skills, gaining experience in different areas of law, and building your network. Attend legal events, seminars, and conferences, and try to connect with legal professionals and experts in your field. You can also consider taking additional courses, obtaining specialized certifications, or pursuing higher education to enhance your credentials.

Finally, remember that getting into a tier-1 law firm is highly competitive, and there may be several factors beyond your control. However, if you work hard, gain experience, and build your network, you can increase your chances of achieving your career goals.

(For further details, kindly refer to Chapter IV point 4.3: What if you are rejected)

54. How can I work for a foreign law firm in India?

NP: The rule to allow Foreign Law firms to practise in India has not yet been implemented, but Indian lawyers can work for foreign law firms in India or overseas. Here are some ways you can work for a foreign law firm in India:

- **Join an Indian law firm with international connections**: Many Indian law firms have international affiliations or alliances with foreign law firms. Joining such a firm can provide you with exposure to international legal work and the opportunity to work with foreign lawyers.

- **Work in the legal department of a foreign company**: Many multinational corporations have legal departments in India staffed with both Indian and foreign lawyers. You can apply for legal positions in these departments to work with and for foreign lawyers.

- **Work as a consultant or legal advisor for a foreign law firm**: While foreign law firms are not allowed to practice law in India, they can hire Indian lawyers as consultants or legal advisors to provide legal advice on Indian law. You can apply for such positions with foreign law firms that have a presence in India.

- **Work as an independent lawyer**: As an independent lawyer, you can provide legal services to foreign clients or law firms in India. You can specialize in areas such as international arbitration or cross-border transactions to attract foreign clients.

It's important to note that while Indian lawyers can work for foreign law firms, they must comply with the rules and regulations of the Bar Council of India regarding foreign law firms' activities in India.

55. Can I practice litigation in any place without the knowledge of the local language? For example, what if I don't understand the Marathi language and want to practice in Mumbai or don't know Tamil and want to practice in Chennai?

NP: Knowing the local language is certainly critical and can be an advantage for Tier II and Tier III cities in India but not Mumbai as it is a cosmopolitan city, and the courts in Mumbai conduct proceedings in English and Marathi. The same is the case in Chennai. However, it's recommended that you have some knowledge of the local language to be able to communicate with clients and understand legal documents written in the local language.

If you don't understand Marathi, it may be a disadvantage for you in some cases as you may have difficulty in communicating with clients or understanding certain legal documents. However, if you are fluent in English, you can still practice litigation in Mumbai as English is the primary language of communication in the legal profession in India.

56. Which field of law has the most scope for growth in the future?

NP: Law is a continuously developing field. The scope for growth in any field of law is dependent on various factors such as economic, political, and social factors. Additionally, the demand for lawyers in a particular field can vary depending on the location and the specific needs of the market. The following are the fields with the most scope for growth:

- Data Science/Artificial Intelligence/Big Data/Cloud Computing and laws related to technology-driven business models like EdTech/ FinTech/ E-Retail.

- Intellectual Property Law: This includes patents, trademarks, copyrights, and trade secrets.

- Cyber Law: This includes areas such as data privacy, cyber security, and e-commerce.

- Environmental Law: This includes areas such as climate change, renewable energy, and sustainability.

- International Law: This includes areas such as international trade, investment, and human rights.

- Healthcare Law: This includes areas such as healthcare regulation, medical malpractice, and healthcare compliance.

- Dispute Resolution/Alternate Dispute Resolution

57. How to choose a law firm to apply for a job?

NP: Choosing a law firm to apply for a job can be a really daunting task. Here are some tips to help you select the right law firm for you:

- Do your research about firms and also partners with whom you wish to work; and then, decide which one suits the best for your need.

- Consider your career goals and long-term plans. See how they align with the law firm you are choosing.

- Talk to current and former employees of different law firms to get a clear idea of the work-related aspects.

- Attend networking events in order to stay updated with ongoing developments.

- Consider the location which is more comfortable for you.

- Look for diversity and inclusion to gain more extensive working experience.

(For further details, kindly refer to Chapter IV point 4.1: First placement)

58. Is it mandatory to do an LL.M. after LL.B.?

NP: No, it is not mandatory to do LL.M. after LL.B. LL.M. is a postgraduate program that offers advanced legal education in a specific area of law, and it is not a requirement to become a lawyer in India. In India, after completing an LL.B. degree, one can appear for the Bar Council of India exam and become a practising lawyer. However, an LL.M. can be helpful in providing specialized knowledge and skills in a particular area of law and may be required for certain job positions or career paths. Higher degrees always help you to build your credentials.

59. Is it necessary to specialise in a particular field after graduation?

NP: No, it is not necessary to specialise in a particular field after graduation in law. However, specializing in a particular field can provide you with an edge over other candidates and can increase your chances of getting a job in that field. It can also help you gain expertise and knowledge in a specific area of law, making you a valuable asset to law firms and organizations that specialize in that area. Additionally, specialization can lead to higher salaries and better job opportunities in some cases. However, it ultimately depends on your personal interests, career goals, and the job market in your area.

60. What is better- an LL.M. in India or abroad?

NP: Deciding whether to pursue an LL.M. in India or abroad depends on your individual career goals and personal circumstances. Just because your friends have gone abroad and have got an opportunity to work in international law firms doesn't mean it may suit you or you may even get the same opportunity. Most importantly, doing LLM just is no guarantee that Indian law firms would rate you on any higher ranking. So don't feel in any manner inferior if you cannot go abroad for LLM. I keep repeating that your competition has to be with yourself and not your colleagues from college.

Here are some factors to consider:

- **Quality of education**: LL.M. programs in both India and abroad can provide high-quality legal education. However, the curriculum, faculty, and resources may vary by institution.

- **Specialization**: Consider the area of specialization you want to pursue and whether the LL.M. program offers courses in that area.

- **Career opportunities**: Consider the career opportunities available after completing the LL.M. program. If you plan to work in India, an LL.M. from an Indian university may be more beneficial, while an LL.M. from a foreign university may provide more opportunities for working abroad.

- **The cost of pursuing an LL.M.** can vary greatly between India and abroad. Tuition fees, living expenses, and other costs should be factored in when making your decision.

Ultimately, the decision between pursuing an LL.M. in India or abroad depends on your individual goals, circumstances, and preferences. You should consider the above factors and research various LL.M. programs to determine which one is the best fit for you.

61. Will I earn more if I go abroad for work?

NP: It is possible to earn more by working abroad as a lawyer, but it also depends on various factors such as the country you are working in, the type of law you practice, the size and reputation of the law firm you are working for, and your level of experience and expertise.

In some countries, such as the United States or the United Kingdom, lawyers may earn significantly more than lawyers in India or other countries. However, the cost of living in those countries may also be higher.

62. What does a law firm look for in an applicant?

NP: It depends on the law firm and any immediate vacancy they may have. When a law firm is considering an applicant, they typically look for the following:

- Strong academic record

- Relevant work experience

- Strong writing and research skills

- Attention to detail

- Interpersonal skills

- Demonstrated commitment to the firm

63. Can I become a lawyer if I have a criminal record?

NP: The Bar Council of India (BCI) Rules set out certain eligibility criteria for individuals seeking to enrol as advocates in India. The BCI Rules require that a person seeking enrollment must be of good character and must not have been convicted of an offence involving moral turpitude.

Therefore, having a criminal record could potentially impact your eligibility to become a lawyer in India. However, each case is evaluated on a case-by-case basis, and the final decision rests with the Bar Council of India.

If you have a criminal record and are interested in pursuing a career in law, it is advisable to seek guidance from the Bar Council of India or consult with a lawyer who can provide more specific advice based on the details of your situation.

64. I have done LL.B. more than 10 years ago; how can I start my career in law now?

NP: If you completed your LL.B. more than 10 years ago and have not yet practised law in India, there are still several options available to start your law career in India:

- **Enrol as an Advocate**: You can enrol with your State Bar Council as an Advocate, which will allow you to practice law in India.

- **Pursue an LL.M.**: Consider pursuing an LL.M. degree to update your legal knowledge and skills. This will not only help you in your practice, but it can also enhance your marketability to potential employers.

- **Gain work experience**: Consider gaining work experience by working with a law firm, a legal services company, or a corporate legal department. This will allow you to develop skills and knowledge in your chosen area of law and demonstrate your value to potential employers.

- **Build a network**: This can help you find job opportunities and build your professional reputation.

- **Consider alternative legal careers**: If you are unable to find a job in a traditional law firm or legal practice, consider alternative legal careers such as legal journalism, legal research, legal writing, or teaching law.

Research the legal market in India and stay up to date with industry news to stay informed and identify new opportunities.

(For further details, kindly refer to Chapter IV: Entry into the legal profession)

65. How can I apply for a juniorship in SC after graduating?

NP: If you have recently graduated from law school and are interested in applying for a juniorship in the Supreme Court of India, here are the steps you can follow:

- **Create a resume and a cover letter**: Prepare a comprehensive resume highlighting your academic and extracurricular achievements, as well as any legal internships or other relevant work experience. Draft a customized cover letter that highlights your interest in working in the Supreme Court of India and outlines your skills and experience.

- **Research Supreme Court Juniorship Programs**: There are several Juniorship Programs available in the Supreme Court of India, such as the Court Clerk-cum-Research Assistant, the Law Clerk-cum-Research Assistant, and the Registrar's Trainee Scheme. Research the requirements, application process, and deadlines for these programs.

- **Apply for Juniorship Programs**: Once you have identified the Juniorship Program you want to apply for, submit your application along with your resume and cover letter to the designated authority. Follow the instructions for submitting the application carefully and ensure that all necessary documents are included.

- **Prepare for the interview**: If your application is selected, you may be called for an interview. Prepare for the interview by researching the Supreme Court of India and its current cases, as well as by practising answering common interview questions.

- **Follow up**: After the interview, follow up with the designated authority to inquire about the status of your application. If you are selected, you will receive a letter offering you a position as a Junior in the Supreme Court of India.

It is important to note that competition for Juniorship Programs in the Supreme Court of India is fierce and the application process is highly selective. Therefore, it is important to start preparing well in advance, research thoroughly, and present yourself in the best possible manner.

66. Is it mandatory to get registered with a Bar Council after graduation in order to pursue a career in law?

NP: Yes, it is mandatory to get registered with a Bar Council after graduation to pursue a career as a lawyer in India. The Bar Council of India is the regulatory body that governs legal education and professional practice in India. It is responsible for maintaining the standards of legal education and ensuring the professional conduct of lawyers.

To practice law in India, a person must first obtain a law degree from a recognized law school and then get registered with the State Bar Council where he or she intends to practice.

After registration, a person can practice law in the courts and tribunals of India, subject to fulfilling certain conditions and requirements, such as completing a mandatory period of apprenticeship, passing a qualifying examination, or meeting certain other eligibility criteria.

67. What exactly is an articled clerkship for the Solicitors Exam?

NP: In India, an articled clerk is a person who has completed a law degree and is undergoing a period of practical training under a practising lawyer, known as a "principal". The term "articled" refers to a written agreement or contract between the clerk and the principal, which outlines the terms of the clerkship.

The period of training for an articled clerk in India is typically three years, during which the clerk gains practical experience in various aspects of legal practice, such as drafting legal documents, appearing in court, and assisting with legal research. The training is intended to provide the clerks with a broad understanding of legal practice and prepare them for a career in law.

At the end of the training period, the articled clerk is required to take a qualifying examination, which tests their knowledge and skills in various aspects of legal practice. Upon passing the examination, the clerk becomes eligible to practice law as a licensed lawyer.

(For those who don't know what a solicitor exactly is, I have answered it in a separate question under the "Miscellaneous" chapter.)

(For those who don't know what a solicitor exactly is, I have answered it in a separate question under Chapter VII point 7.6 Miscellaneous)

68. What benefits would I get if I cleared the Solicitor's exam?

NP: The Solicitor's Exam is conducted by the Bar Council of India, and it is a qualifying exam for lawyers who wish to become solicitors. I am a 1991 batch Solicitor and can certainly say that earlier in the 90s, it certainly made a difference in Mumbai if you were a solicitor.

Clearing this exam can offer several benefits, including:

- **Expanded knowledge and expertise:** Since I am a Solicitor, I can say for sure that preparing for the exam is a herculean task! And certainly, would enhance your knowledge and expertise in many laws.

- **Increased legal skills:** The exam is designed to test your legal skills, including research, drafting, and advocacy.

- **Enhanced career opportunities:** Clearing the Solicitor's Exam can open up new career opportunities and increase your earning potential.

- **Professional recognition:** Becoming a solicitor is a significant achievement and can provide you with professional recognition and credibility in the legal community.

69. I have no practical experience; does that mean I won't qualify for a job in a reputed law firm?

NP: Having no practical experience may make it more difficult to get a job in a reputed law firm, but it doesn't necessarily mean that you won't qualify for one. Law firms do look for candidates with an attitude toward learning and work done in law schools, but they also consider other factors such as technical skills, academic qualifications, and relevant extracurricular activities.

If you do not have practical experience, you can try to gain some by volunteering or interning with a law firm or legal organization.

You can also consider taking additional courses or certifications in areas relevant to the type of law you are interested in practising. This can demonstrate to potential employers that you are committed to your career and willing to invest in your education and professional development.

70. What are the options for a Government job after graduation in law?

NP: There are several options for government jobs in India after graduation in law. Some of these options are:

- **Judicial Services**: One of the most popular government job options for law graduates is to become a judge in the lower judiciary.

- **Public Prosecutors**: Law graduates can also work as public prosecutors in various state and central agencies, including the Central Bureau of Investigation (CBI), the Enforcement Directorate (ED), and the National Investigation Agency (NIA).

- **Legal Advisors**: Law graduates can work as legal advisors for various government departments and ministries, providing legal advice and guidance on legal matters.

- **Law Officer in Banks**: Law graduates can work as law officers in various public sector banks and financial institutions, providing legal advice and guidance on legal matters.

- **Law Officer in PSUs**: Law graduates can work as law officers in various public sector undertakings (PSUs), providing legal advice and guidance on legal matters.

- **Academia**: Law graduates can also work as law professors or lecturers in various government-run universities and colleges.

These are some of the popular government job options available for law graduates in India.

71. How to get your first client as a lawyer?

NP: It can seem a little challenging to get your first client, but it is not that difficult. This is like how do I get a first patient as a doctor? If you have always thought of opening up your own practice, I advise you to start building your foundation of prospective clients from your days at the law school itself.

As a fresher, you will majorly get clients from your known circle and references – the bigger the circle, the chance of getting a quick client is more. So, it is important to let people you are known to see your qualities as a lawyer. Try to indulge yourself in their cases when you're still a student/intern. Research their issues and provide them with your unique thoughts. Offer free consultation in order to demonstrate your technical expertise and solution-oriented approach.

Other than that, you may partner with other professionals like accountants, financial planners, or real estate agents who may refer clients to you. Be active on social media platforms like LinkedIn, Twitter, Facebook, etc., to promote your services and share your experience.

Like any other profession, if you are opening your private practice in law, know that its success will majorly depend on your goodwill. So, be smart to present yourself and your skills from the early stages of your career.

72. It is said that your senior helps you to get a few clients when you open up your own practice. Doesn't that make them lose their own business?

NP: Seniors can help you get your own clients by sometimes transferring their own clients to you. When a senior advocate helps a new practitioner get clients, it does not necessarily mean that the senior will lose their own business. In fact, it can be beneficial for both parties.

Firstly, a senior advocate may have a large client base that they cannot serve fully due to time constraints or other reasons. By referring some of these clients to a new practitioner, the senior is able to ensure that the clients receive the services they need while also maintaining a positive relationship with them.

Secondly, a new practitioner may have unique skills, experience, or perspectives that can complement the senior's practice. By working together and sharing with clients, the two advocates can create a more robust and diverse practice, which can be attractive to potential clients.

Finally, building a successful practice often requires networking and building relationships with others in the industry. By helping a new practitioner get started, a senior advocate can establish a positive relationship with the new practitioner and potentially, create opportunities for future collaboration and referral.

In summary, helping a new practitioner get clients can be a win-win situation for both the senior advocate and the new practitioner, as it can lead to a more robust and diverse practice for both parties.

73. I have recently opened up my private practice in criminal law but all I'm able to get are civil cases. If I take them, I'm afraid that I'll only be known as a civil lawyer, but on the other hand, I can't afford to lose my clients at such an initial stage. What can I do?

NP: Firstly, it is important that you have a network of good lawyer friends in different practices because no one lawyer can claim expertise in all these laws for example Civil Laws, Corporate Laws, Criminal Laws, Employment Laws, Co-operative Laws, Property Laws, Tax Laws, Constitutional laws, Rent Act, Consumer Laws, Banking Laws, Laws governing Intellectual Property Rights, Media & Entertainment Laws, Insurance Laws, and Hindu Succession Laws. It is, therefore, important that you know experts in these areas of practice so that when you get any client, you can immediately consult them and provide services jointly with them. It is important for you to tell the client that you are not an expert but would be happy to coordinate the services. In this bargain, you also keep learning and progressing.

This is very much similar to the medical or engineering practice. No one doctor can claim to be a specialised doctor in one aspect of medicine. There are General Practitioners, Surgeons, Heart Specialists, Cancer Specialists, Orthopaedic Surgeons, Paediatricians, Gynaecologists, Neurosurgeons and many others.

8.5 Internships

74. Is it important for law students to take up multiple internships in law firms?

NP: The importance of multiple internships for law students during their academic studies cannot be overstated. These internships serve as crucial gateways to real-world legal experience, bridging the gap between theoretical knowledge and practical application. They provide students with the opportunity to observe the inner workings of the legal system, from court proceedings to the nuances of legal drafting and client interactions. Each internship, whether in a law firm, a corporate legal department, or with a practising advocate, offers a unique perspective and a chance to explore different areas of law. This exploration is vital in helping students identify their areas of interest and specialization. Furthermore, internships are a valuable platform for networking, allowing students to build connections with professionals in the field. These relationships can be instrumental in securing future job opportunities and mentorship. In a competitive field like law, the diverse experiences and skills gained through multiple internships can significantly enhance a student's employability and readiness to embark on a successful legal career.

Many law schools require students to complete a certain number of internship hours in order to graduate, and some internships may offer academic credit towards a law degree.

(For further details, kindly refer to Chapter III point 3.3: Internships)

75. Is it okay if I only focus on my grades and curriculum instead of doing any internships? Will that help me get a good job right after graduation?

NP: My straight answer is a BIG NO. While good grades and a strong curriculum can certainly help you in your job search as a law graduate, it's generally recommended that you also gain practical experience through internships or other relevant work experience.

Internships provide law students with the opportunity to gain practical experience and develop important skills that can be valuable in their careers. Through internships, you can network with professionals in the legal field, gain exposure to different areas of law, and get a better understanding of what type of legal work you may be interested in pursuing after graduation.

Overall, while good grades and a strong curriculum are important, it's not just advisable but a 'must' to gain practical experience through internships or other relevant work experience in the legal field to enhance your job prospects after graduation.

76. When to have my first internship?

NP: The timing of your first law internship can depend on various factors, such as your academic standing, personal circumstances, and career goals.

In general, law students usually start looking for internships after their first year of law school. However, some students may choose to wait until their second or third year to gain more knowledge and experience in the field.

It's important to keep in mind that internships can be competitive, and it may take some time to secure a position. You may want to start researching and applying for internships several months in advance of when you hope to start.

Please refer to Chapter Law in Law School for more information on Internships.

77. How/where can I apply for my first internship when I have zero practical experience?

NP: Applying for your first legal internship in India when you have zero practical experience can seem challenging, but there are still several ways you can go about it:

- Check with your law school's career services office/placement cell: Most law schools in India have career services offices that can help you identify potential internship opportunities and provide guidance on how to apply for them.

- Look for internships online: There are many websites and job boards that specialize in legal internships in India, such as Internshala, LetsIntern, and Lawctopus. You can also check the websites of law firms and legal organizations to see if they have any internship openings.

- Contact law firms and organizations directly: If there is a particular law firm or legal organization that you are interested in, you can reach out to them directly to inquire about internship opportunities. Be sure to research the firm or organization beforehand and tailor your application to their specific needs and requirements.

Remember to be proactive and persistent in your search, and to make sure your resume and cover letter are well-written and tailored to each opportunity you apply for. Good luck!

(For further details, kindly refer to Chapter III point 3.3: Internships)

78. What is better – exploring all the possible fields in various internships OR sticking to just one field to gain a solid practical knowledge in it?

NP: Both options have their advantages, and the right choice depends on your career goals and personal preferences. Here are some points to consider:

<u>Exploring all possible fields of law through internships can be beneficial because:</u>

- It can help you identify the area of law that you enjoy the most.

- It can help you gain a broad range of skills and experiences, which can be useful in different fields.

- It can help you build a diverse network of contacts in the legal field.

<u>On the other hand, sticking to just one field to gain solid practical knowledge in it can be beneficial because:</u>

- It can help you become an expert in that field, which can make you more marketable to potential employers.

- It can help you develop deep connections with mentors and colleagues in that field.

- It can help you gain a greater understanding of the legal issues and nuances specific to that area of law.

Ultimately, the choice between exploring different fields or sticking to one depends on your career goals and interests. If you are unsure about which field of law to pursue, exploring different fields through internships can help you gain a better understanding of what you enjoy. If you have a clear idea of the field you want to specialize in, focusing on gaining practical experience in that field can help you develop your skills and knowledge.

79. How are NGO internships helpful in law?

NP: Interning at a non-governmental organization (NGO) can be very helpful for law students and aspiring lawyers. Here are some reasons why:

NGOs often work on issues related to human rights, social justice, and environmental protection. As an intern, you will get hands-on experience working on legal issues related to these areas. This experience can help you develop a deeper understanding of the legal challenges faced by marginalized communities and how the law can be used as a tool for social change.

NGOs often provide interns with opportunities to work on legal research, drafting legal documents, and attending court hearings. This experience can help you develop practical legal skills and gain a better understanding of how the legal system works.

NGOs often work across different countries and legal systems. As an intern, you may have the opportunity to work on legal issues related to international law and gain a better understanding of how different legal systems work.

Interning at an NGO can demonstrate your commitment to social justice and public service, which can be an asset when applying for legal jobs in the future. It can also demonstrate your practical legal skills and experience, which can set you apart from other applicants.

80. What are judicial internships and what are their benefits?

NP: Judicial internships in Indian courts provide law students and young lawyers with the opportunity to work alongside judges, observe court proceedings, and gain practical experience in the legal field. Here are some ways in which judicial internships in Indian courts can benefit you:

- **Exposure to the legal system:** Judicial internships provide a unique opportunity to observe the functioning of the legal system up close. You will be able to witness court proceedings and understand how judges make decisions.

- **Practical legal experience:** As a judicial intern, you will have the opportunity to work on legal research, drafting legal documents, and attending court hearings. This experience can help you develop practical legal skills and gain a better understanding of how the legal system works.

- **Networking opportunities**: Judicial internships provide an opportunity to build relationships with judges and legal professionals. This can be beneficial for your future career prospects, as it can lead to job opportunities and mentorship.

- **Enhance your resume**: Judicial internships are highly valued in the legal profession and can be a valuable addition to your resume. Employers view judicial internships as evidence of your dedication to the legal profession and your interest in pursuing a career in the judiciary.

- **Insights into the legal process**: Judicial internships provide an opportunity to gain insights into the legal process from the perspective of judges. This can help you develop a deeper understanding of legal issues and how they are resolved in court.

Overall, judicial internships in Indian courts can provide you with valuable legal experience, exposure to the legal system, and networking opportunities that can be beneficial for your future legal career.

81. What if I get an internship but don't get good-quality of work assigned to me?

NP: If you find that you are not getting good quality work assigned to you during your legal internship, there are several steps you can take to address the situation:

- Talk to your supervisor, explain your interests and ask if there are any specific projects you can work on that would better match your interests and abilities.

- Offer to help with other projects or tasks. This can show your initiative and willingness to take on new challenges.

- Seek out additional learning opportunities outside of your assigned tasks. Attend court hearings, observe meetings, and talk to other lawyers and interns to learn more about their work.

- It can be frustrating when you are not getting the kind of work you want, but it's important to remain positive and professional. Approach each task with enthusiasm and professionalism and be open to learning from your experiences.

- If you have tried to address the situation and are still not getting the kind of work you want, it may be time to re-evaluate whether this internship is the best fit for you. Consider talking to your career services office or a mentor for advice on how to proceed.

Remember, internships are an opportunity to learn and gain experience, even if the work is not exactly what you had hoped for. Stay open to learning and growing, and use this experience as a stepping stone for your future legal career.

82. How can I prepare for my interview for an internship?

NP: Preparing for a legal internship interview requires a combination of research, preparation, and practice. Here are some tips to help you prepare:

- Research the law firm and the practice of the partner concerned under whom you wish to work.

- Go through the website of the law firm and speak to HR to understand the process, if possible.

- Prepare responses to common interview questions.

- Review your resume and cover letter.

- Dress professionally and be punctual.

- Follow up after the interview.

By following these tips, you can feel more confident and be prepared for your legal internship interview. Good luck!

(For further details, kindly refer to Chapter IV point 4.1: First placement)

83. How to be good at research work?

NP: Being good at legal research work requires a combination of skills, knowledge, and practice. Here are some tips to help you improve your legal research skills:

- Before beginning any research project, it's important to have a clear understanding of what you're looking for and how you're going to find it. Develop a research plan that outlines your research question, the sources you'll consult, and the search terms you'll use.

- When conducting legal research, it's important to use reliable sources that are accurate and up-to-date.

- Conduct a thorough search of all relevant sources, including online databases, print materials, and other resources. Don't rely solely on a single source or database, as this can lead to gaps in your research.

- When conducting legal research, it's important to critically analyse and evaluate your sources to determine their relevance and reliability. Consider the author's credentials, the date of publication, and any biases or agendas that may be present.

- Keep track of your research using a system that works for you, such as a spreadsheet or note-taking app. This will help you stay organized and ensure that you don't miss any important information.

- Legal research is an ongoing process and it's important to stay up-to-date on new developments in the law. Subscribe to legal publications to stay informed.

By following these tips, you can improve your legal research skills and become a more effective researcher.

84. How can I be sure to deliver good quality work to my seniors?

NP: Before beginning any assignment, make sure you understand the task at hand. Clarify any questions or uncertainties with your senior so that you can approach the work with confidence.

- Attention to detail is critical in the legal profession. Double-check your work for errors and inconsistencies, and make sure that you have followed all instructions and guidelines.

- Organize your work in a clear and logical manner, using headings, bullet points, and other formatting techniques to make it easy to read and understand.

- Use reliable sources and make sure that your research is accurate, up-to-date, and relevant to the assignment.

- Analyse the legal issue at hand thoroughly, taking into account relevant statutes, case law, and other authorities. Consider different perspectives and potential arguments to ensure that your work is comprehensive and well-rounded.

- Seek feedback from your seniors to ensure that your work meets their expectations. Use their feedback to improve your work and ensure that you are meeting their needs.

By following these tips, you can ensure that you are delivering high-quality work to your seniors in your legal internship. This will help you build a positive reputation and advance your career in the legal profession.

85. Is it beneficial to work as an Intern in a single law firm in the final year of my course in order to land a job there?

NP: Interning in a single law firm during your final year of law school can be beneficial if you are interested in working for that firm after graduation. It can provide you with an opportunity to gain hands-on experience, develop professional relationships with lawyers and staff, and demonstrate your skills and work ethic to potential employers. By interning in a single law firm, you can also gain a deeper understanding of the firm's culture, values, and practice areas, which can help you determine if it is the right fit for you.

However, it is important to note that interning in a single law firm is not the only way to land a job there. Many law firms also recruit through on-campus interviews, job fairs, and other recruitment events and may consider candidates who have interned at other firms or have gained relevant experience in other ways.

86. Internships are discouraged in my college. Is it true that theoretical knowledge is more important than practical experience?

NP: While theoretical knowledge is certainly important, practical experience through internships can also be extremely valuable for law students. Through internships, students can gain hands-on experience in a real-world legal setting, such as a law firm or a legal aid organization. This experience can help students understand how the law is applied in practice and can give them a better sense of what they might like to specialize in as they progress in their legal careers.

In addition, internships can provide opportunities for networking and making professional contacts, which can be important for finding employment after graduation. Internships can also be a way to explore different areas of law and gain exposure to different legal specialities.

Therefore, while theoretical knowledge is important, it is generally a good idea for law students to seek out internships or other opportunities for practical experience in the legal field.

8.6 Miscellaneous

87. Which law field is currently in demand in India?

NP: In India, there are several law fields that are in demand and have good job opportunities. Here are some of the most popular law fields in India:

- **Corporate Law:** Corporate law involves advising companies on their legal rights, obligations, and responsibilities. This field is in high demand as more companies are expanding and require legal assistance to comply with regulations.

- **Intellectual Property Law:** Intellectual Property (IP) law involves protecting the rights of individuals and companies with regard to their intellectual property, such as trademarks, patents, and copyrights. With the rise of technology and creative industries, IP law is in high demand.

- **Tax Law:** Tax law involves advising individuals and companies on tax-related matters, such as compliance, planning, and dispute resolution. With the complex tax system in India, tax lawyers are in high demand.

- **Cyber Law:** Cyberlaw involves advising individuals and companies on legal issues related to the internet and technology, such as data privacy, cyber security, and e-commerce. With the increase in online transactions, cyber law is becoming more important.

- **Environmental Law:** Environmental law involves advising individuals and companies on legal issues related to the environment, such as pollution, conservation, and sustainability. With the growing concern for the environment, environmental lawyers are in demand.

These are some of the most popular law fields in India, but there are many other areas of law that also have good job opportunities. Ultimately, the demand for a particular law field may vary depending on the location, industry, and other factors.

Going forward ESG and SDG would be in demand.

88. What exactly is litigation?

NP: Litigation is the process of resolving disputes through the court system. It involves the representation of clients in court proceedings, such as trials, hearings, and motions, and the use of legal procedures and strategies to achieve a favourable outcome.

The litigation process typically begins with a complaint or petition filed by one party against another, which sets out the allegations and legal claims. The defendant then has the opportunity to respond, either admitting or denying the allegations and presenting any counterclaims.

After the pleadings are filed, the parties engage in the discovery process, which involves the exchange of evidence and information relevant to the case. This may include depositions, written interrogatories, requests for documents, and other forms of discovery.

The next stage of litigation is typically pre-trial motions, in which the parties ask the court to rule on specific legal issues, such as the admissibility of evidence or the dismissal of certain claims.

If the case is not resolved through settlement or alternative dispute resolution, it will proceed to trial, where the parties present their evidence and arguments to a judge or jury. The court will then issue a judgment or verdict, which may be appealed to a higher court.

Overall, litigation is a complex and time-consuming process that requires a thorough understanding of the law, legal procedures, and courtroom strategies. It is typically handled by experienced litigators, who may specialize in a particular area of law or type of litigation.

89. What is a Lawyer, Attorney, Advocate, Solicitor, Barrister, and a Legal Practitioner?

NP: In India, a lawyer, attorney, advocate, solicitor, barrister, and legal practitioner all refer to professionals who are trained and licensed to provide legal advice and represent clients in legal proceedings. However, there are some differences in their specific roles and qualifications:

- **Lawyer:** The term "lawyer" is a general term that refers to anyone who has a law degree and is licensed to practice law in India. Lawyers can provide legal advice, draft legal documents, and represent clients in court.

- **Attorney:** An attorney is a lawyer who is authorized to act on behalf of someone else, such as a client, in legal matters. In India, the term "attorney" is not commonly used, but it may be used interchangeably with "lawyer."

- **Advocate**: An advocate is a lawyer who represents clients in court, particularly in the higher courts such as the High Court and the Supreme Court. To become an advocate, a person must have a law degree and pass the All-India Bar Examination.

- **Solicitor**: A solicitor is a type of lawyer who typically works in a law firm and provides legal advice to clients. In India, the term "solicitor" is not commonly used, but it may be used to refer to lawyers who specialize in corporate or commercial law. Students need to clear the exam and articleship in order to practise as a Solicitor.

- **Barrister**: A barrister is a type of lawyer who specializes in court advocacy and provides legal opinions to clients. In India, the term "barrister" is used to refer to lawyers who are members of the Bar Council of India and have been called to the Bar in England and Wales.

- **Legal Practitioner**: A legal practitioner is a generic term that refers to any person who is licensed to practice law in India, including lawyers, advocates, and solicitors.

Overall, the terms used to refer to lawyers in India can vary depending on the context and the specific legal profession of the individual in question.

90. Is it important to be fluent in the English language in order to become a successful lawyer?

NP: English is the language of the legal profession in India, and fluency in English is certainly important for success as a lawyer. Most legal education and practice in India are conducted in English and proficiency in the language is required for drafting legal documents, presenting arguments in court, and communicating effectively with clients and colleagues.

However, the Constitution of India recognizes 22 languages and various state governments have designated their own official languages. As a result, courts in India also function in the local language, depending on the state or region.

In my years of experience, I have observed that students who come from vernacular medium schools face an added struggle to be proficient in English. While fluency in English can provide an advantage in the legal profession, it is possible for non-native speakers of English to succeed as lawyers with hard work, dedication, and focused efforts to improve their language skills. Legal education and professional development programs may offer language support to help students and professionals improve their English proficiency.

91. What are Tier-1 law firms? What are the other types of law firms?

NP: Tier-1 law firms are generally considered to be the largest and most prestigious law firms in a given market or region. These firms typically have a global presence, offering legal services across multiple practice areas to clients ranging from large corporations to government agencies and high-net-worth individuals. They are known for their expertise, resources, and high-quality legal services.

Other types of law firms include:

- **Mid-sized law firms** - These firms typically have fewer lawyers than tier-1 firms and offer legal services across a narrower range of practice areas. They may also have a more regional or local focus.

- **Boutique law firms** - These firms specialize in one or a few niche areas of law, such as intellectual property, tax, or environmental law. They may be smaller in size but are known for their expertise in their specialized areas.

- **Virtual law firms** - These firms operate entirely online and offer legal services to clients through remote communication channels.

- **In-house legal departments** - These are legal departments within corporations or other organizations that provide legal services exclusively to their own company or organization.

- **Solo practitioners** - These are individual lawyers who practice law on their own and may offer a range of legal services or specialize in one area of law.

92. Do I need to be good with basic computer skills like Word, PPT, etc.?

NP: As a lawyer, it is very helpful to have some level of proficiency with computers and technology. In today's digital age, many legal tasks and processes are conducted using computers and software. For example, you may need to draft legal documents, review and organize large amounts of electronic documents, conduct legal research using online databases, and communicate with clients and other lawyers through email or video conferencing.

Having good computer skills can also help you be more efficient and productive in your work, allowing you to complete tasks more quickly and accurately. In addition, being able to use technology effectively can make you a more attractive candidate to potential employers or clients.

However, it is not necessarily a requirement to be an expert in all aspects of technology as a lawyer. You may be able to work with support staff or technology specialists to assist you with more complex or specialized tasks. The most important thing is to have a basic level of computer literacy and be willing to continue learning and adapting to new technologies as they arise.

93. Is it true that you need to have at least some amount of legal knowledge to lead a good life irrespective of whether you practise law or not?

NP: While having some legal knowledge can be helpful in certain situations, it is not necessarily essential for leading a good life. However, there are certain basic legal concepts that can be useful for everyone to understand in order to protect their rights and make informed decisions.

For example, knowing your basic rights as a citizen, such as the right to free speech or the right to a fair trial, can help you make informed decisions and protect yourself in various situations. Understanding basic contract law can also help you make informed decisions when entering into agreements with others, whether in a personal or business context.

While it may not be necessary to have extensive legal knowledge, having a basic understanding of key legal concepts and processes can be helpful in certain situations and can contribute to leading a more informed and empowered life.

94. Why are NLUs so preferred by students?

NP: National Law Universities in India are highly respected and recognized for their academic excellence, hard work, and contributions to the legal field.

National law universities were established to promote excellence in legal education and research in India, and they have played a significant role in shaping the legal landscape of the country. These institutions attract some of the brightest and most motivated students in the country and provide them with rigorous academic training, practical skills, and opportunities to engage with the legal profession.

The success of national law universities in India can be seen in the fact that their graduates have gone on to occupy important positions in the judiciary, legal academia, and the legal profession in India and abroad. Many national law universities have also produced influential legal scholars and have contributed significantly to the development of Indian jurisprudence.

These institutions have made significant contributions to the legal education and profession in India and they continue to be highly respected and valued by students, academics, and legal professionals alike.

95. Does pursuing an LL.B. help in getting a promotion in careers like banking, etc.?

NP: Obtaining an LL.B. degree may help in getting a promotion in certain careers like banking, but it ultimately depends on the specific job requirements and qualifications.

In some banking or financial roles, having legal knowledge and expertise can be an advantage. For example, individuals with a legal background may be better equipped to handle complex regulatory and compliance issues or may be able to provide legal advice to clients.

However, it's important to note that the value of an LL.B. degree may vary depending on the industry and the specific job requirements.

Additionally, pursuing an LL.B. degree can provide valuable transferable skills such as critical thinking, research, and analytical skills that may be beneficial in a range of careers.

96. Is law considered a respectable choice of career in India?

NP: Yes, law is generally considered a respectable and prestigious career choice in India. The legal profession has a long and rich history in India, and the legal system plays an important role in upholding the rule of law and protecting the rights of individuals.

There are several factors that contribute to the high level of respect and prestige associated with a career in law in India. First, the legal profession is highly regulated and requires a rigorous academic and professional qualification process. This ensures that lawyers are well-trained and knowledgeable about the law, which, in turn, enhances their reputation and credibility.

Second, lawyers in India are often seen as advocates for justice and fairness and are expected to uphold high ethical standards in their practice. This makes the profession highly respected among the general public, who rely on lawyers to protect their rights and interests.

97. How can I build a good CV?

NP: Building a good CV in the legal profession requires a combination of education, experience, and skills. Please refer to Chapter V for a detailed discussion.

(Kindly refer to Chapter III point 3.7: Preparing CV for internships)

98. What is the requirement to become a Judge?

NP: To become a judge in India, one must meet certain eligibility criteria and follow a specific career path. Here are the basic requirements to become a judge in India:

- **Educational Qualification:** The candidate must have a Bachelor's degree in Law (LLB) from a recognized university.

- **Work Experience:** The candidate aspiring to become a Judge at a High Court or the Supreme Court must have practised as an advocate in a High Court or Supreme Court for at least 10 years.

- **Age Limit:** The candidate must be between the ages of 35 and 45 years at the time of appointment.

- **Selection Process:** The selection of judges in India is done through a judicial service exam conducted by the respective state's Public Service Commission or the Union Public Service Commission (UPSC) for appointment in the higher judiciary.

The appointment of judges is made by the President of India on the recommendation of the Chief Justice of India in consultation with the senior judges of the Supreme Court. After the appointment, the candidate is required to undergo training at the National Judicial Academy or the State Judicial Academy, depending on the level of appointment.

It is important to note that the process of becoming a judge in India is highly competitive and requires a combination of academic excellence, legal knowledge, and experience. Additionally, a judge is expected to be impartial, ethical, and committed to upholding the rule of law, and must possess the necessary qualities to serve as an effective and fair adjudicator.

99. There are various fields in law. But are there any fields that can only be practical in urban cities and not rural areas and vice versa?

NP: Yes, there are some fields of law that are more relevant or in demand in urban areas compared to rural areas and vice versa.

For example, in urban areas, there may be a higher demand for lawyers practising in areas such as real estate law, intellectual property law, and corporate law, due to the concentration of businesses and commercial activities. On the other hand, in rural areas, there may be a higher demand for lawyers practising in areas such as agricultural law, environmental law, and land law, due to the prevalence of farming and natural resource issues.

However, it's important to note that many fields of law are relevant in both urban and rural areas, such as family law, criminal law, and civil litigation. Additionally, with the increasing prevalence of remote work and technology, some fields of law that were previously more urban-centric may become more accessible to rural areas as well.

100. How do lawyers decide their fees? On which factors does the payment depend? Also, what qualities make Senior Advocates the most expensive lawyers in India?

NP: There is no hard and fast rule about the fees that lawyers charge in India as compared to the Western World, where mostly, the fees are charged based on time spent on an hourly basis based on seniority. In India, the hourly rate system is now getting accepted in major cities and for foreign clients. The other method is to quote lumpsum fees could start from Rs. 25,000/- to Rs. 50,000/- as one-time consultation fees and later, as the matter develops, a lawyer's charge.

For transactional work in Corporate/Banking/Securities Law, the charges depend upon the scope of work for example for legal due diligence of a mid-sized company a law firm could charge around Rs. 6 lakhs to 10 lakhs for legal due diligence and approximately the same fees for documentation.

Chapter 9

Revamping Legal Education: Steps for Law Schools

Indian law schools have a crucial role in enhancing legal education for their students. It's about taking meaningful actions to ensure that law students receive the most relevant, comprehensive, and practical training. Here, I have recommended a few necessary changes and improvements law schools could consider preparing future lawyers for the challenges and opportunities of the legal world.

- **Creating Awareness:** Law Schools/Law Colleges organise free lectures of eminent lawyers/Judges/partners from law firms for the open public to create awareness about legal studies and put this discourse on their YouTube Channels; or in collaboration with Junior Colleges or Schools Standard XII.

- **Informal Study Circle:** Law Schools should encourage the formation of informal study circles on various topics and, in fact, institutionalize the process to incept a culture of open discussions, sharing insights and robust teamwork.

- **Internship Cell to connect with Law firms and Industry** – Law schools should form a robust internship cell under the guidance of any faculty member under the supervision of any experienced human resource personnel along with a team of enthusiastic students. The internship cell should keep a detailed database of students with the facility to update their CVs on a regular basis; information about law firms (various practices), individual partners (their specializations), institutions like (SEBI, RBI), senior lawyers, judges, tribunals, and their contact details. I would also like to recommend that the internship cell should establish connections with business houses via various Industry Forums like ASSOCHAM, Indian Chamber of Commerce, Indian Merchants Chamber or international chambers operating in India and structure an internship program.

- **Peer Groups for Research:** Ideally, A law school should encourage forming small peer groups of students under the guidance of external faculty to discuss topics and issues regularly. These discussion groups are like assembling a think tank of budding legal minds. These discussions are not just conversations; they're incubators for ideas, fostering a collaborative learning environment where every opinion adds a new dimension to your understanding.

- **Discourse on New Industry Domains:** Law schools should establish programs that consistently expose students to new industry domains. By engaging industry experts, academics, and thought leaders, these programs can offer a rich, multi-faceted learning experience. Regular interactions with professionals from various fields not only broaden the student's understanding of the legal landscape but also keep them abreast of emerging trends and challenges.

- **Compulsory Moot Courts:** Moot Courts aren't mandatory in Indian law schools, leading many students to bypass this opportunity. Unfortunately, it's often later in their careers that they recognize the missed value of participating in moot courts. This hesitation to engage often stems from a lack of confidence, an area where the support and guidance of the law school could make a significant difference. Effective handholding by the faculty can nurture students' confidence, encouraging them to take up moot court activities. I am of the strong view that a certain number of moot courts be made compulsory for every law student and should not be optional at all.

- **Legal Clinics:** Many law schools now offer legal clinics, where students work on real cases under the supervision of practicing attorneys. This hands-on experience can range from providing legal assistance to underserved communities to working on high-profile public interest cases.

- **Simulation Exercises**: Simulated negotiations, mediations, and trial advocacy exercises are becoming more common. These simulations often involve role-playing scenarios that mimic real-world legal situations, offering students a practical, immersive learning experience.

- **Externships and Fellowships**: Externships with law firms, courts, government agencies, and non-profit organizations offer on-the-job training. Fellowships might involve working on specific legal research projects or with advocacy groups, providing deeper insights into specialized legal fields.

- **Innovation and Technology Labs:** Some law schools have set up labs where students can work on legal technology and innovation projects, such as developing legal apps, exploring artificial intelligence in law, or working on access to justice technology projects.

- **Transactional Law Competitions:** For students interested in corporate law, transactional law competitions provide an opportunity to draft and negotiate business transactions, offering practical experience in a field where traditional moot courts may not.

- **Policy and Legislative Drafting Workshops:** These workshops allow students to work on drafting actual policy documents or legislation, giving them a taste of the legislative process and the intricacies involved in crafting legal texts.

- **International Arbitration Training:** With the rise in international trade and cross-border disputes, training in international arbitration, including participation in related competitions, provides valuable exposure to global legal practices.

- **Legal Hackathons and Design Thinking Workshops:** These events encourage students to use creative problem-solving skills to address legal challenges, often involving interdisciplinary collaboration.

- **Pro Bono Projects:** Engaging in pro bono work offers students the chance to work on real cases while serving the community, gaining practical experience and a sense of the societal role of legal professionals.

About the author

Nitin Potdar, formerly a Corporate Partner at J. Sagar Associates from 2005 to 2024, now practices independently as a Corporate & M&A Lawyer & Strategic Advisor, leading a focused team of young lawyers. With a commitment to delivering high-quality, tailored legal services across diverse industries, Nitin combines deep legal expertise with strategic insight to meet each client's unique needs.

Professional Background and Expertise

Specializing in Mergers & Acquisitions, Corporate Restructuring, Joint Ventures, and Private Equity Deals, Nitin has a proven track record of successfully guiding multinational corporations into the Indian market and assisting family businesses with succession planning. His extensive experience includes advising on Foreign Direct Investments and navigating complex regulations, helping clients from the US, UK, Germany, and Japan thrive in India.

Recognition and Thought Leadership

Nitin was recognized as the 'Most Influential & Significant Lawyer in 2019' by the Asia Pacific Legal 500. Chambers & Partners noted his active M&A and foreign direct investment practice, praising his expertise in advising inbound foreign clients. He is a sought-after speaker at conferences and seminars on the Takeover Code, M&A, and Joint Ventures.

Mentorship and Education

Through his initiative, Conversations with Nitin Potdar, he actively mentors emerging legal professionals. Earlier, Nitin authored a book that presents a far-sighted scientific theory—The GPS Paradigm for M&As and JVs—designed to help companies across various sectors thrive, not merely survive. This book empowers founders, business leaders, CEOs, and professionals, including investment bankers, lawyers, and tax advisors from different generations, to navigate their future business journeys effectively. Simply put, it's for those mavericks who aspire not just to drive change, but to be the change.

He started his career with Carwford Bayley & Co (1991), became Partner Amarchand Mangaldas (1999), Joined JSA (2005 – 2024).